Marketing

Success

Stories

by Hollis Hatfield Weishar

Personal Interviews
with 66 Rainmakers

ABA American Bar Association
Law Practice Management Section

Cover design by Gail Patejunas.

Nothing contained in this book is to be considered as the rendering of legal advice for specific cases, and readers are responsible for obtaining such advice from their own legal counsel. This book and any forms and agreements herein are intended for educational and informational purposes only.

The Section of Law Practice Management, American Bar Association, offers an educational program for lawyers in practice. Books and other materials are published in furtherance of that program. Authors and editors of publications may express their own legal interpretations and opinions, which are not necessarily those of either the American Bar Association or the Section of Law Practice Management unless adopted pursuant to the By-laws of the Association. The opinions expressed do not reflect in any way a position of the Section or the American Bar Association.

Library of Congress Catalog Card Number 97-70253
ISBN 1-57073-399-6

01 00 99 98 97   5 4 3 2 1

Discounts are available for books ordered in bulk. Special consideration is given to state bars, CLE programs, and other bar-related organizations. Inquire at Publications Planning and Marketing, American Bar Association, 750 N. Lake Shore Drive, Chicago, Illinois 60611.

Contents

About the Author

Hollis Hatfield Weishar began working with lawyers as a marketing consultant in 1986 in Kansas City, Missouri. She owned and operated her marketing consulting practice for more than ten years and specialized in working for law firms, accounting firms, and architectural firms, primarily in the areas of practice development, strategic planning, client relations, and professional training.

Ms. Weishar has consulted for many professional service firms throughout the United States, including Lathrop & Gage, KPMG Peat Marwick Accountants, and HOK Architects in Kansas City, Missouri; The Frank Lloyd Wright Foundation in Scottsdale, Arizona; and The Modrall Law Firm and Sutin Thayer & Browne in Albuquerque, New Mexico. Before establishing her consulting practice, Ms. Weishar was the director of marketing for a sixty-five member architectural firm in Kansas City, Missouri.

More recently, she worked as the director of marketing for Hinckley, Allen & Snyder, a 120-lawyer, regional New England law firm with offices in Boston, Massachusetts, and Providence, Rhode Island. In 1997, Ms. Weishar joined the Law Firm Development Group (LFDG) as a marketing consultant. LFDG is a Boston-based marketing, consulting, and training organization that works with firms throughout North America. LFDG assists firms in creating and implementing marketing training, strategic planning, business develop-ment, and client feedback programs.

Ms. Weishar has a bachelor's degree in marketing from Central Missouri State University and presently serves on the board of the New England Region of the National Law Firm Marketing Association. She has been a speaker on marketing, staff training, business development, and client relations for groups throughout the United States.

She resides in East Greenwich, Rhode Island, with her husband, Greg Weishar, and their two children, James and Robert.

Acknowledgments

This book has sixty-six authors. While I developed the original concept, served as the facilitator for the project, performed the research on the law firms, interviewed the lawyers, crafted many of the individual success stories, and managed the overall project, the real authors of this book are the lawyers who devoted their time and energy to share their ideas and make this project come alive.

I would like to thank all of the individuals who contributed to this project.

Hollis Hatfield Weishar

Foreword

The ABA Section of Law Practice Management has published a number of books for lawyers who want to improve their marketing skills. Our readers tell LPM Publishing that marketing is the subject about which they are the most interested. So when Hollis Weishar proposed that she interview lawyers all over the country and distill their marketing wisdom into short vignettes in their own words, we were enthusiastic about adding this book to our marketing line.

Ms. Weishar is an experienced legal marketing consultant. She has succeeded in capturing marketing stories from rainmakers in all fifty states—from solo practitioners to partners in mega-firms, young lawyers to seasoned practitioners—in varied practice areas. The book is a resource tool for every lawyer's personal marketing strategy. You will discover that each of these lawyers, whatever his or her circumstances, has something valuable to share and does so in a direct and candid manner.

For greater ease of use, the stories are divided into five parts: Building Relationships; Developing a Marketing Program; Niche Marketing; Client Service; and Referrals. Although the book can be read straight through, no story is more than a few pages long, so you can read a few stories at a time and work those tips you are comfortable using into your personal marketing plan. Whether you read one story a day, a week, or a month, we believe that you will find a wealth of practical advice. You may even return in the future to those stories that do not currently seem to apply to your practice, and find that they have acquired a new relevance. You will want to keep this book close at hand for ready reference and inspiration.

LPM Publishing is proud to add *Marketing Success Stories: Personal Interviews with 66 Rainmakers* to its popular marketing line, which includes *Women Rainmakers' 101+ Best Marketing Tips* by Theda Snyder; *The Lawyer's Guide to Marketing on the Internet* by Gregory Siskind and Timothy Moses; *The Last Frontier: Women Lawyers as Rainmakers* by Judith Grubner; and *Do-It-Yourself Public Relations: A Success Guide for Lawyers* by David Gumpert. We trust that you will find the advice contained in these success stories to be useful and rewarding additions to your marketing repertoire.

Robert J. Conroy
Judith L. Grubner
Co-Chairs
LPM Publishing

How to Use This Book

This book is a collection of sixty-five marketing success stories. The stories are organized into the following five parts:

1. Building Relationships: One Client at a Time
2. Developing a Marketing Program: Ideas That Work
3. Niche Marketing: Positioning for Success
4. Client Service: Maintaining and Growing Clients
5. Referrals: Making a Name for Yourself

These stories are grouped into these parts based on the overall theme of each story, but many communicate a comprehensive approach to setting up a successful marketing program. The stories are presented so that each can stand alone, which should enable the reader to pick up and enjoy this book again and again. I believe that this book will be a valuable resource for busy lawyers, law firm marketing professionals, and law school students who are interested in learning more about how to market legal services. The techniques presented here can be used to market any lawyer, in any size firm, in any geographic region, at any level of experience, and with any practice specialty. With each success story, I have included brief information about the lawyer and his or her firm, including office locations, number of lawyers, and major areas of practice. The marketing concepts presented here are tested and proven. Whether you are interested in learning about setting up a client survey program, planning your strategy for a "beauty contest," or creating a firmwide marketing program on all levels, this book contains helpful advice and a how-to approach for you.

Introduction

In 1985, I became interested in helping lawyers do a better job of marketing themselves. I was working as the director of marketing for a large architectural firm in Kansas City, Missouri, and began approaching local law firms to hire me in a marketing position. Several firms were very interested, but only one firm, Gage & Tucker, agreed to take the big step and hire me to assist them. The executive committee was not ready to hire an in-house, full-time director of marketing, so I was hired as a consultant and worked on a project basis, creating a new firm brochure, developing a client newsletter, and updating the individual mailing lists of fifty lawyers. That was my initiation into law firm marketing. Needless to say, law firms today practice in a much more competitive environment and are much more strategic in their thinking about marketing.

Ten years later, in 1995, I began writing this book for the Law Practice Management Section. At the time, I was working closely with Roberta Cooper Ramo while doing marketing consulting work for her firm, Modrall, Sperling, Roehl, Harris & Sisk in Albuquerque, New Mexico. Roberta was about to become president of the American Bar Association, and she introduced me to the concept of writing a marketing book for the Law Practice Management Section. I spent time talking with lawyers and members of the LPM Publishing Board, discussing my idea of compiling a book made up of the real-life "marketing success stories" of lawyers. My work with lawyers had taught me that they are generally very busy people and are not very enthusiastic about attending formal training programs or reading textbooks in an effort to improve their practice development skills. What my experience had *also* taught me, however, was that lawyers were *very* interested in listening to their peers tell tales of marketing success. So a concept was born.

I devoted more than a year to interviewing lawyers about their marketing successes. Their stories, contained here, are fascinating and diverse. Of course, many share the basic belief that marketing begins and ends with providing quality client service, but, as you will discover by reading the individual stories, each lawyer has a unique way of delivering this service. As I developed the manuscript, I tried to include a representative sampling of lawyers from throughout all regions of the United States. I have profiled male and female lawyers, lawyers who are solo practitioners, and lawyers who are partners in the largest firms across the country. I included lawyers in a wide range of practice areas. Some of the lawyers are just beginning their careers, many are more experienced, a few are famous, but most are not, and they all share one common trait—they love to market and they have had success with their efforts.

This book is simply a collection of personal stories, communicated as they were told to me, with some light copyediting for grammar and consistency. It provides an inside look at how successful lawyers market themselves, their practice specialties, their firms, and their profession. Writing this book has provided a wonderful learning experience for me. People often ask me what I have learned from this experience. I would like to summarize here what interviewing sixty-six lawyers taught me about marketing.

Marketing in law firms is still *gaining* in importance. Lawyers are more enthusiastic than ever about marketing. I was surprised to learn that lawyers still have a growing interest in marketing. The lawyers who I interviewed for this book have very diverse practices, but they share a common thread—their techniques work. The sixty-six lawyers profiled in this book are, I believe, a representative sampling of a large and growing contingent out there.

Lawyers are very willing to share their good ideas with other lawyers. I think that traditionally lawyers have been unfairly accused of being "territorial" or "protective" of their clients and their ideas. The lawyers I interviewed for this book were more than willing to share all their marketing secrets and successes—without hesitation. In fact, out of all the lawyers I contacted to participate in this project, only two refused to publicize their techniques. Interestingly enough, both of these lawyers were in very large New York City law firms, practicing in one of the most competitive markets in the country.

Large firms typically have adopted an institutional approach to marketing. I learned that firms with more than three hundred lawyers have developed *very* formalized programs and tend to market on a "macro" level, while medium-sized and small firms focus on marketing individual lawyers and practice specialties. I also observed that large firms have organized marketing committees for decision making, while smaller firms expect individual lawyers to take on the responsibility and have the initiative to market themselves.

Successful marketers and rainmakers have one thing in common—they understand the power of relationship building. Very few of the lawyers who I interviewed told tales of success from using impersonal or "credibility" marketing approaches such as brochures, newsletters, or advertising. A majority of the lawyers focus their marketing approach on building lasting relationships with clients, prospective clients, and referral sources. It *does* all come down to who you know, not what you know.

Effective marketing may require a combination of tactics. Although building relationships was cited as the most powerful tactic, no one single tactic works for everyone. The most successful lawyers called upon a variety of techniques to build and enhance relationships with clients and prospects and referral sources, including community service, speaking, writing, and golf.

It takes time, attention, planning, money, and commitment. All the lawyers I interviewed communicated to me that they devote considerable amounts of time and energy to marketing. Many of these lawyers have prepared a written "marketing plan" to follow for implementation. I sensed that even if they did not have a detailed, written plan, each one had a marketing "plan" in mind that provided overall direction. Almost all of them reiterated the fact that effective marketing requires a planned, consistent, and ongoing effort.

Providing a quality legal product and excellent service is still the number-one marketing technique. Each lawyer I interviewed had a unique marketing approach. One consistent theme, however, came through—that marketing begins with the delivery of a quality legal product and ends only when the client is completely satisfied.

To be successful, you must first know your client, your market, and your area of expertise. A majority of the lawyers profiled in this book communicated the importance of having an adequate knowledge base about the client. The message came through loud and clear. If a lawyer doesn't take the time to establish what he or she is selling, and to listen to the client and learn the client's business, no amount of marketing will be successful.

Marketing strategies should be focused on existing clients first. A few of the lawyers interviewed actually enjoyed "cold calling," but a majority relied on their existing client base and network of contacts to refer new business to them. Lawyers are beginning to realize that they *can* generate new business from their existing clients if they *ask for it.* "Team" marketing of clients involving several lawyers from different practice areas also appears to be gaining in popularity, particularly in large firms.

Finally, lawyers need to enjoy their work. All of the lawyers who provided a success story for this book mentioned that they truly enjoy their work. I believe that this may be the most important marketing technique shared by this group. The bottom line is that unless a lawyer communicates enthusiasm, all other marketing efforts will fail.

Hollis Hatfield Weishar

To be effective in any marketing activity, a lawyer must be perceived as someone who understands what it is to do lawyering with a high level of integrity. This lawyering must be integrated in the commercial setting . . . you must have a complete understanding of the business of the person you are representing; and you must be perceived as an individual who is open, creative, and communicative. Having an active and respected role in the community is also very important.

Roberta Cooper Ramo
Modrall, Sperling, Roehl, Harris & Sisk
Albuquerque, New Mexico
President, American Bar Association
1995–1996

PART 1

Building Relationships: One Client at a Time

The Million-Dollar Contract

Lawyer: James A. Durham

Firm: The Law Firm Development Group

Locations: Boston, Massachusetts

**Practice
Areas:** Practice Development Consulting for Law Firms

If there is a way to summarize the business development success story I am about to share, it is to call it
the "Million-Dollar Contract." Whenever you are wondering
whether you should help someone out just a little bit (perhaps with a free bit of advice or a shoulder to cry on), you
should think about the "Million-Dollar Contract."

Although I was fortunate to have spent three years in the
business world before going to law school, I still arrived at a
big Boston firm as an associate like most—without a clue.
Back in the early 1980s, believe it or not, there was not a
great deal of emphasis on identifying future rainmakers. In
fact, significant efforts to develop business as an associate
were essentially discouraged. What I discovered, however,
was that you do not actually have to make dramatic efforts
to develop solid business—you just need to be aware of
people's needs and do as much as you can to help them.
Specifically . . .

I had been at a big law firm for about six months when I was assigned to a matter involving a three-way dispute between two business partners and a major athletic manufacturer. One of the individuals (our client) was a nice young man who had never before been involved in any kind of litigation. He was referred to our firm by an out-of-state lawyer, so he had no previous contacts or relationships with any of our lawyers. The partner handling the matter was one of our more sensitive attorneys, but he had principal responsibility for managing a rather complex case, so he was not in as good a position as I to focus on the client's *personal* pain. In the process of assisting in this case, I came to know the client quite well.

I was particularly aware of the fact that the client was confused by the legal system, and threatened by the process, so I made an extra effort to help him cope. Whenever possible we would talk about something other than the case to calm his nerves, and I would make a point to try to give him some clear perspective on the case's posture. It turned out that he was in the tennis business, and since I played tennis, I suggested that we play some evening. It seemed like a great way to break down some barriers, ease the tension of the litigation, and get to know each other better.

Without giving you the agonizing details, I will simply say that we played tennis fairly regularly and we continued to develop our relationship during the course of the litigation. One day, during a break in a deposition, the client took out a small, standard-form architecture contract and asked if I would take a quick look at it. He was putting an addition on his house and this contract related to the plans. He admitted that he would not ordinarily ask a lawyer to look at something like this, but since we had reached a good comfort level, he thought it made sense to have me take a quick look.

Believe it or not, even a first-year lawyer (particularly one who has had three years of prior business experience) can read a standard-form contract and offer some meaningful advice. I gave him my analysis and suggested that we could have someone with more experience look at it, but I told him it really did not seem necessary under the circumstances.

He clearly appreciated my basic advice and the down-to-earth approach I took to the contract. The fact that I was helping him with something that was important to him personally reflected favorably on me and my role as his lawyer.

I started visiting his place of business on occasion to learn more about his business. I learned that he was involved in some significant and exciting projects that involved a number of contracts and the prospect of substantial financial reward (and exposure). I also learned that he had not had his agreements (which were a complex series of letters and amendments) reviewed for many years. As a result of our relationship, he was receptive to my suggestion that I review the agreements—just to give him some sense of the soundness of the contracts. Our personal connection, and my demonstrated interest in his business, created an atmosphere of trust.

After reviewing a series of documents, which stretched over a span of about seven years, I realized that there were, in fact, a lot of important business and legal issues that had been ignored. However, based on habit and good fortune, no major problems had arisen. I pointed out the problem areas to my client but suggested that he do nothing to "rock the boat." I advised him that we could revise the various agreements as they expired, and thereby begin the process of standardizing the agreements and plugging some of the holes.

Again, he appreciated the fact that I did not come in with legal guns blazing and suggest that he overhaul his defective contracts and disturb relationships that had been working, notwithstanding the fact that the contracts were horrific.

Over the course of the next several years I worked with him on all aspects of his business. Not only did we revise his contracts, but I assisted him in drafting and preparing business proposals, negotiating his lease, and evaluating new opportunities. Our relationship continued to grow.

I suggested that he work with one of our estate planning attorneys, who prepared a sophisticated estate plan. Other lawyers in the firm represented him in connection with the purchase and sale of his house and a suit relating to the installation of some landscaping.

Also, when a couple of particularly difficult legal issues arose at the client's parent company in New York, they called me instead of their usual counsel. Based on my work for the subsidiary, they realized that I had a good understanding of their business, and my relationship with the subsidiary made me trustworthy. This initial work for the parent led to further new business with parent.

Have I mentioned the other referrals that flowed from this client relationship? The client was so pleased with the attention I paid to his personal and business concerns that whenever anyone was looking for a lawyer, guess who he recommended? Two of the more significant clients I brought in during my first three years of practice were referred to me by this client.

This relationship was responsible for several hundred thousand dollars of business in my first five years of practice. More importantly, perhaps, when I had an opportunity to become an entrepreneur and a sports agent, it was this client's willingness to continue to work with me on a retainer basis that provided the financial bridge I needed to be able to leave a large law firm and venture into a sports law career.

I represented the client on virtually all of his legal matters while trying to start my sports marketing career. At the end of the next two years the client moved to the home office in New York, where they already had an in-house counsel. (That person was not only a good lawyer but was also family and lived in New York—something with which I could not compete!) This meant that he had good legal counsel right under his nose.

Nevertheless, over the years we continued to refer business opportunities to each other. I assisted him in developing some proposals for expanding his business, and he provided me with valuable insight and business opportunities. I referred people to him with products he might market. He referred people to me who might need counsel or business advice in Boston.

He also provided me with advice in the development of a product that might be sold through direct mail (something with which he has considerable experience), and he even expressed a willingness to invest in the project. Several years later I helped him find a commercial real estate broker to locate office space in, of all places, my little town (that's right, he was thinking of moving back to Boston), and I made it clear that I was prepared to help him in any way possible.

It has been nearly ten years since we first met, and my client recently took over the parent company. One of the first things he did was hire me to provide some independent advice on an important business transition matter.

I am confident in saying that over the course of the past decade something approaching "a million dollars" has probably changed hands or moved around (from someone to somewhere) as a direct result of this client relationship. I cannot help but think back on that scene in the reception area back in 1983, when this nervous fellow asked me if I would take a quick look at his home improvement contract.

Out of that contract grew one of my most valued and meaningful personal and professional relationships.

In summarizing what made it happen, I can say with confidence that it was my sincere caring for this client's well-being. It was not my legal skills, my business savvy, or my dazzling personality that led to a successful long-term relationship. He knew I cared for him and his business; we developed a mutually beneficial relationship; and he knew I could be trusted. That, in my mind, is what every person wants from a lawyer.

The $5.95 Client

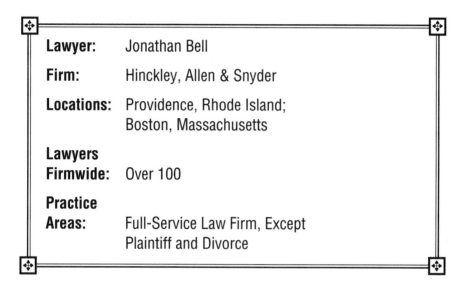

Lawyer:	Jonathan Bell
Firm:	Hinckley, Allen & Snyder
Locations:	Providence, Rhode Island; Boston, Massachusetts
Lawyers Firmwide:	Over 100
Practice Areas:	Full-Service Law Firm, Except Plaintiff and Divorce

Good marketing begins and ends with taking a personal interest in clients.

One potential corporate client of mine had a need for estate planning. I referred the client to one of my partners who specialized in this area and personally sat in on the initial meeting to make the necessary introductions. Before the meeting began, I chatted with the client's wife about her interests. She mentioned that she was very interested in reading a particular book. So immediately following the meeting, I went to the bookstore and purchased a copy of the book for her (for a total cost of $5.95). I sent the book to the client's wife with a handwritten note, and within a month the client had transferred all his corporate files to my firm. By taking the time to build a personal relationship with this client's wife, and then following up on our discussion, I was able to generate additional business.

Don't Ignore the
Support Staff!

Lawyer: Davis H. Carr

Firm: Boult, Cummings, Conners & Berry, PLC

Locations: Nashville, Tennessee

Lawyers Firmwide: 66

Practice Areas: General Practice; Civil Trial and Appellate Practice before All State and Federal Courts; Administrative Agencies and Commercial Arbitration Forums; Antitrust and Trade Regulations; Banking and Finance; Bankruptcy; Commercial Finance; Communications; Construction; Corporations; Employment and Labor; Entertainment; Environmental; Estate Planning and Administration; Family Law; Health Care; Information; Intellectual Property; Land Use Regulation; Litigation, including Commercial and Business and Personal Injury Litigation; Mergers and Acquisitions; Municipal Finance; Municipal Law; Music and Entertainment; Partnerships; Pensions and Employee Benefits; Publishing; Real Estate Development and Syndication; Securities; Federal, State, and Local Taxation; Tax-Exempt Organizations; Telecommunications; Utilities.

Early in my practice, I was a banking lawyer who did all types of transactional work. Then, ten years ago, my largest bank client was sold. Suddenly I was no longer a bank lawyer, and I had to decide just what type of lawyer I wanted to be in the middle of my career. Mergers and acquisition work was what I enjoyed the most, so I began marketing myself as an M & A lawyer.

First, I came up with a plan. My initial goal was simply to build name recognition in the community. I wanted every lawyer and important businessperson in Nashville to know who Davis Carr was. I learned who the local lawyers were and spoke to them at every opportunity. I always made sure that I used their names ("Hello, Mr. Smith"), because when someone calls you by name, you remember that individual. I attended every business reception or event I could and introduced myself to everyone I could. I began to serve on boards and became actively involved in a number of organizations. Within three years, I had gained quite a bit of name recognition. Obviously, it is a long, continuous process, but over time this technique has been successful for me as one method of developing business.

A more personal marketing technique I use is to pay attention to and be pleasant to all people, especially the support staff who work with my clients. I make it a point to call secretaries by name and ask how they are doing. This makes the individuals feel a little more important, since they are often ignored by others.

I have one marketing success story that is an example of how this really paid off for me. There is a major manufacturing company in Nashville that has become a six-figure paying client of mine because of a referral from a secretary. The owner of the company had a daughter who married a lawyer. The lawyer eventually was hired by the company to serve as in-house counsel. While this individual was a very competent lawyer, he had limited experience in dealing with some of the problems that this company was facing. He had one particular complex leasing problem that he needed to hire an experienced lawyer to help him solve. He mentioned to his assistant that he needed to find a good lawyer with leasing experience. She was not aware of any local lawyers with this type of experience, but she placed a call to her friend, the bank president's secretary, and asked if she knew any lawyers. The bank was one of my large clients, and I had taken time over the years to develop a good working relationship with the president's secretary. This secretary replied that the assistant should call Davis Carr because "he knows everything." The truth is that I did not have any expertise in leasing law, but my partner did, and we landed this major client—all because I took the time to be nice to the bank president's secretary.

I also spend time building relationships with business owners in the community. It is a fact that eight out of ten people who own a business will sell it eventually. So I target these business owners as my potential clients. I make it a point to get to know them before they are interested in selling, so that once they decide to sell, they will know who to call immediately. Generally, I meet these business owners through my community involvement. Once I have met them, I call them and invite them to lunch. By taking this approach, I am not making a "cold" call. I make sure that they know that I am a lawyer and that I specialize in buying and selling businesses. This marketing activity has been successful for me. I have received many referrals from individuals because business owners have a network developed with each other. When one is interested in selling, they will, generally, make a call to another business owner and ask if he or she knows a good lawyer.

All in all, it is a relationship business. You have to develop and maintain relationships on all levels to be successful at marketing and developing new business.

Expand Your Horizons

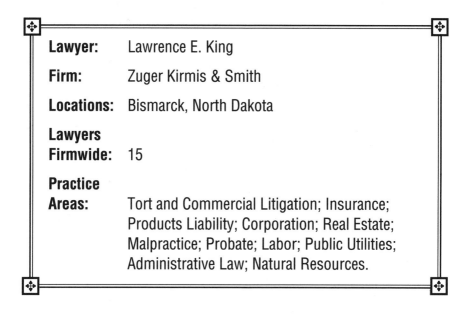

Lawyer: Lawrence E. King

Firm: Zuger Kirmis & Smith

Locations: Bismarck, North Dakota

Lawyers Firmwide: 15

Practice Areas: Tort and Commercial Litigation; Insurance; Products Liability; Corporation; Real Estate; Malpractice; Probate; Labor; Public Utilities; Administrative Law; Natural Resources.

The law firm with which I am presently associated practices extensively in the insurance defense law area. Basically, we have a very well-established clientele within this industry. In North Dakota, there are only about 1,600 licensed attorneys. Since there is a fairly small client base, we have to be very competitive. Like any other lawyer, I have found that it can be difficult to expand and grow your practice under these circumstances. Most potential clients out there have already developed a legal relationship.

When I began practicing with my present firm, I was new to this part of North Dakota. I was interested in expanding my practice to develop more commercial work, specifically in the area of bankruptcy. I felt that I could effectively represent debtors, and there appeared to be a market for bankruptcy work in this area.

One day I got a call from a woman who was working with a nonprofit entity, helping individuals with consumer debt counseling. Many of these individuals were facing potential bankruptcy. The woman was preparing a report with a statistical analysis of bankruptcy information for our state. She called me in an effort to generate some information for her report. I agreed to assist her, and I spent some time performing an analysis for her. After I compiled all the data, I went to pay her a visit and meet with her personally. By spending the extra time to walk over to her office and meet with her, we got to know each other and now we refer a considerable amount of work to one another. She will routinely refer to me individuals who have real bankruptcy filing needs, and I will refer to her potential clients who are not candidates for bankruptcy but who could benefit from credit counseling.

By taking the extra time, at no charge, to assist this woman in gathering bankruptcy statistical information, I was able to form a comfortable working relationship. I still find it difficult to believe that other lawyers did not already have a referral relationship in place with this credit counseling organization. I believe that as young lawyers we overlook simple ways to reach and attract new clients. By understanding the interrelationships of various businesses and agencies and establishing ties with those entities, one is able to break into a new area of law and develop a practice.

Emergency Service, Twenty-Four Hours a Day, Seven Days a Week

---

Lawyer: Jay Frontino

Firm: Bates, Meckler, Bulger & Tilson

Locations: Chicago, Illinois

Lawyers Firmwide: 40

Practice Areas: All Areas of General Commercial Litigation; Insurance; Reinsurance; Excess and Professional Liability Coverage; Labor and Employment; Product Liability and White-Collar Criminal Litigation and Counseling.

I developed a highly successful top-end client who was deeply involved in the writing of environmental impairment liability policies (EILPs) ranging from $5 million to $60 million limits. The purpose of the policies was to insure corporations for past and present environmental episodes (spills, etc.). Over a four-year period, I developed this client into a $12 million relationship. I did this by preparing and sending this client a manual on EILPs and positioning myself as a legal expert in this area. To enhance this position, I included in the manual directives on how to handle environmental "emergencies." My name, office telephone number, and home telephone number were included, with instructions that I would be available twenty-four hours a day, seven days a week to answer questions or provide assistance should any emergencies arise.

One Saturday morning I received a phone call at home from this client requesting that I attend a meeting in Pittsburgh on Monday to deal with an environmental emergency. I immediately began researching the issue on Saturday afternoon. On Sunday I flew to Pittsburgh and met with the client. On Monday I had a meeting with the insured's general counsel. The insured had made a demand on my client to pay $18 million for an environmental "episode" that occurred one year earlier. I advised the client not to pay the $18 million, which was the right decision, resulting in a savings of $18 million and a new client relationship that brought me one hundred additional cases and billings of $3 million annually.

Marketing through Performance

Lawyer: Charles R. Coulter

Firm: Stanley, Lande & Hunter

Locations: Muscatine, Iowa; Davenport, Iowa;
Wilton, Iowa

Lawyers Firmwide: 18

Practice Areas: General Civil and Trial Practice; Corporation;
Business; Banking; Taxation; Securities; Tax-
Exempt Financing; Labor; Employment Discrim-
ination; Administrative; Creditor Bankruptcy;
Agricultural Law; Insurance Defense; Personal
Injury and Property Damage Law; Pension and
Profit-Sharing; Real Estate; Probate; Estate
Planning; Charitable Trusts and Foundations
Law.

Muscatine County, Iowa, needed a new county jail, and this required a public referendum and formation of a joint city-county authority. I was deeply involved in the referendum and was hired to form the authority. Because the county had no available staff, I served as de facto project manager for some time, oversee-ing the organizational aspects of the project, including meeting agendas and environmental, property acquisition, financing, and political issues.

One of the authority's commissioners was president of a bank in a small city in the county. We worked closely together on the project and he became impressed with my organiza-tional skills and timely performance. A couple of years into the project, he approached me and asked whether our firm was accepting new business clients. Of course, we were.

We now provide substantial legal work for the bank. The president has also referred a large oil distributor to us, and we have provided organizational and tax work for this client. Other members of the bank's board of directors have hired us to provide sophisticated estate planning work.

Overall, we have successfully expanded our client base because we performed in a highly organized manner and on time in the county jail project.

Whatever It Takes to
Win the Client

Lawyer: David L. Johnson

Firm: Baker & Daniels

Locations: Indianapolis, Indiana; Fort Wayne, Indiana; South Bend, Indiana; Elkhart, Indiana; Washington, D.C.

Lawyers Firmwide: Over 200

Practice Areas: General Practice; Administrative; Antitrust; Appellate; Business and Commercial; Computer; Construction; Corporate; Creditors' Rights and Reorganization; Employee Benefits; Employment; Energy; Environmental; Estate Planning and Administration; Family; Federal and State Tax; Financial Institutions; Food and Drug; Government Services; Health Care; Insurance; International Law; Legislative; Litigation; Municipal; Patent, Trademark, and Copyright; Products Liability; Public Utilities; Real Estate; Securities; Sports Law; Tax-Exempt Organizations; Zoning and Land Use Law.

I am a great believer that marketing is very important to a lawyer's practice, but I am not a huge fan of the "wholesale" process of client development. Good clients come from building relationships—and it helps to be in the right place at the right time, which is what happened to me a few years ago.

I had developed a practice in the public finance area. I learned through the grapevine that United Airlines was looking to work out a deal with a city somewhere in the United States to locate a new Maintenance Operations and Overhaul Center. When I first became aware of the project, United was looking at more than one hundred cities. Then I heard that United's selection had been narrowed down to ten cities, then to four, and that Indianapolis was still in the running. I became more and more interested. Then Indianapolis was chosen. It was at that point that every lawyer in the city also became interested in the project.

I decided to try to learn more about the project, since it would involve the types of financings that fall within my area of practice. United was also researching the Indianapolis public finance law firm market. Events converged one Friday morning in late October 1991 when I received the telephone call I had been hoping for—requesting a meeting with me that very afternoon in United's Chicago offices. I tried to find out United's priorities and process for selecting counsel, but there was really no time to pull together any type of a full or well-choreographed firm presentation. So I decided to try to make a virtue out of necessity, and I determined that I would just go talk to United's general counsel in an informal fashion for a first interview. What I did not count on was the weather throwing me a curveball. The temperature suddenly dropped forty-five degrees on that Friday, and the Indianapolis Airport closed because of problems with runway icing. Ironically, I had no choice but to drive to a meeting with an airline. And I knew that near

Mach I speed would be required, since I had nearly two hundred urban miles to cover in less than four hours. It was the worst drive of my life, but it resulted in one of the best clients of my legal career.

Once I arrived, I talked with the United Airlines' general counsel for almost an hour, and I felt a good chemistry building between us. I was delighted, and somewhat stunned, to learn that I had been selected to serve as coordinating outside counsel for United Airlines in the negotiation and implementation of two agreements with the State of Indiana and Indiana local governmental entities. Ultimately, these agreements would provide more than $300 million in cash, tax, and other financial incentives for United to locate a state-of-the-art aircraft maintenance facility in central Indiana, scheduled to cost nearly $1 billion and to employ at least 7,500 when completed by the year 2004. Certainly, it was not my average Friday.

For me, the real effort in marketing to this important client came after the initial selection decision, as I attempted to expand this single transaction with United Airlines into an ongoing client relationship. As any lawyer knows, it can be difficult to turn a transaction into a client. But the effort must begin with seeking to provide true service. Our offices were the site of all of the incentive agreement negotiations and we were therefore obliged to turn our firm into a Wall Street law firm overnight. We worked on a twenty-four-hour-a-day basis for a month, complete with twenty-four-hour copy and food service to handle this mammoth project.

It was a hectic but wonderful beginning to a strong relationship with a justifiably demanding client. We ended up working with United Airlines on all of the contracting relationships associated with the Indianapolis project, developed standard construction contract documents, and negotiated United's new comprehensive facility lease with the Indianapolis Airport. Four years later, our firm continues to represent

United Airlines on all Indiana issues. About eighteen months ago, our firm also began advising United Airlines on facility financing issues arising for United at airports across the United States—in many cases, issues similar to those we have confronted here. Thus, we are pleased today to be doing significant work for United Airlines on a national level. Of course, we do all our traveling on United Airlines!

I believe that United Airlines has found that its relationship with our firm makes sense. Our rates are not as high as other firms, and yet I think that we can still effectively compete in a national market and deliver the level of service and attention that United Airlines deserves.

They are very good people to work with. United Airlines has exposed us to many new challenges and has caused me and others in the firm to take our respective practices in some very different and exciting new directions. Out of our relationship with United Airlines, and because of our firm's involvement in this very visible project, Baker & Daniels is now involved with the whole issue of economic development incentives in Indiana and throughout the United States. Owing to the significance of the United Airlines project and other subsequent (and smaller) incentive transactions in which we have played a major role, our firm today is viewed as a national leader in the emerging field of economic development incentives and public-private partnerships.

Overall, I believe that my public finance background, a small amount of planning and positioning, and a large amount of good fortune all placed me and my firm in the right place at the right time to secure this very important client. This success story is just another example of how, as a lawyer, you have to do whatever it takes to meet your client's needs—even if it means driving for four hours through an ice storm!

Beauty Contests Work

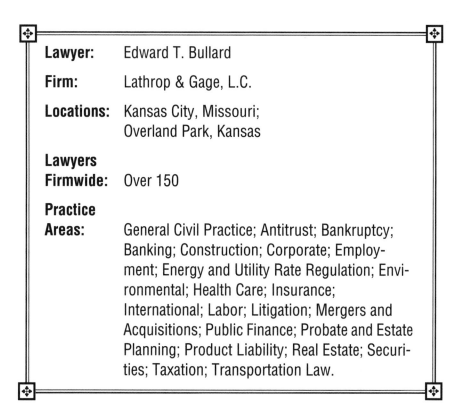

Lawyer: Edward T. Bullard

Firm: Lathrop & Gage, L.C.

Locations: Kansas City, Missouri; Overland Park, Kansas

Lawyers Firmwide: Over 150

Practice Areas: General Civil Practice; Antitrust; Bankruptcy; Banking; Construction; Corporate; Employment; Energy and Utility Rate Regulation; Environmental; Health Care; Insurance; International; Labor; Litigation; Mergers and Acquisitions; Public Finance; Probate and Estate Planning; Product Liability; Real Estate; Securities; Taxation; Transportation Law.

You never know where the business is going to come from. Every lawyer has opportunities to refer a piece of business to a colleague in another firm because of a legal or business conflict. When last confronted with a request for a referral due to a perceived business conflict, I decided to go after the business myself.

I have done business for a number of years with a client in the solid waste management business. One of my contacts in this company went to work for a growing competitor. We kept in touch after he made the move, and one day he called for a favor. He needed to hire a lawyer who could handle a major environmental project in a neighboring state. His company was anxious to hold a "beauty contest," and he wanted me to suggest several firms in the area that might have the capabilities for the representation. He said he suspected that neither his former nor current employer would consent to my firm handling this project because they were competitors. I asked him if he would give me until the end of that week to convince both companies that our firm could effectively represent his current company in this matter without compromise to either business.

I then contacted a vice president of my existing client to plead the case that no *legal* conflict existed to preclude the engagement—only a technical *business* conflict. Even though he understood the difference, he nevertheless declined to consent to the firm representing his competitor. I persisted and called him twice again. Finally, he agreed that if I could convince his company's general counsel, he would agree. The general counsel was far more receptive to the idea and agreed. My next hurdle was to convince the company with the environmental matter to include our firm in the beauty contest. Based on our previous relationship, my contact agreed to allow us to submit a written proposal.

We were now in the beauty contest. We knew that at least two other firms—the Midwest office of a West Coast firm and another Kansas City firm, with whom my contact had a very positive previous experience—were involved. The potential client solicited written proposals from each of us. Our firm assembled a standard brochure, along with a second document profiling a suggested team of lawyers, hourly rates, and an offer to provide periodic budgets. The information included with the standard brochure highlighted the firm's relevant experience in the form of an extensive summary of completed and ongoing similar engagements (protecting client privileges, of course). I followed up the submittal with two conference calls, which included two of my partners from the proposed team (since I had little expertise in the area) to explain our experience. We were advised that we made the first cut. The prospective client invited several firms to come to its home office to make oral presentations about their capabilities and proposals. I requested that our firm present last for two reasons: (1) it would give us more time to prepare and (2) the potential client would have already heard the competition, allowing us to be graded against them. We could respond to the various issues raised by the earlier interviews.

In preparing for the presentation, we decided to learn everything about the company and the decision makers. Before even attempting to resolve the initial business conflict, we did our homework to determine if this potential client was even one we wanted to pursue. We obviously concluded that it was! We collected news clippings, obtained the company's most recent Form 10K filing, learned who was on its board of directors, where all its operations were located, where it intended to expand, and discovered as much as possible about the company's legal needs. We also learned who would be interviewing us and discovered that they were not only the decision makers but also the individuals who would be supervising our legal services. We sought to discover likely fears and frustrations they encountered with respect to lawyers (e.g., cost predictability and containment, fear of being embarrassed by lack of expertise) and were prepared to address each and every one of them. We next researched all Environmental Protection Agency public records with respect to the subject site and those relating to problems at other facilities in the area.

Our next step was to suggest a social agenda before the presentation. A team of two lawyers traveled to the potential client's home office the day before the interview. We had dinner with two of the interviewers the evening before our interview and learned more about the potential representation and their perceptions of the company's needs.

The next morning, we made our presentation. We were joined by a third lawyer from the proposed team. A fourth lawyer was to join us but was unable to do so owing to the weather. We offered to include him by telephone, but the prospective client thought it unnecessary. At the conclusion of the meeting, the client stated that our qualifications looked good but they also wanted a nontraditional fee arrangement that encouraged a timely and efficient handling of the engagement. In today's marketplace, we are finding clients who are much more aggressive with respect to alternative fee requests. Accordingly, we came prepared to discuss potential nontraditional fee arrangements, ranging from straight discounts on standard hourly rates to those that made the firm more of a partner with the client with respect to the proposed engagement. Our preparation enabled us to determine very specifically in our discussions what would best suit this particular company's needs. We followed up our meeting with a written proposal offering a discounted hourly rate combined with a percentage of the remediation costs recovered from third parties. The percentage was weighted to encourage an early resolution and recovery. We apparently were the only firm that offered this type of fee arrangement.

Ultimately, we were chosen for the work, and the client who came to us for referrals owing to a perceived business conflict has became a valued client of our firm on this environmental matter and others. I believe that several components aided us in getting the business: (1) we were able to promptly turn a request to provide a referral into an opportunity to bid for the business; (2) we researched the company and all its players to learn as much as possible about each of them and about the prospective client's business; (3) we attempted to be interviewed last; (4) we added a social element to be better prepared for our presentation; and (5) most important, we were prepared for and answered the client's needs. The company wanted a law firm that not only had the technical expertise to handle the matter but was also responsive, understood the company's business and financial needs, and structured a fee arrangement in response to both. We were successful in obtaining a valued new client while keeping our existing client.

Trust Is Critical

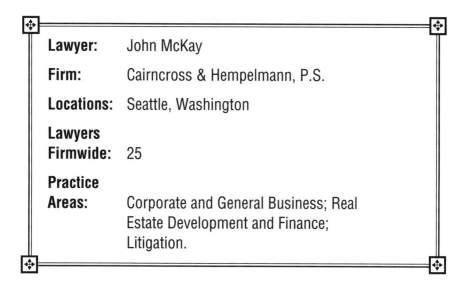

Lawyer: John McKay

Firm: Cairncross & Hempelmann, P.S.

Locations: Seattle, Washington

Lawyers
Firmwide: 25

Practice
Areas: Corporate and General Business; Real
Estate Development and Finance;
Litigation.

Relationships based on trust are critical to marketing effectively. Focus on establishing trust relationships between (1) you and your fellow lawyers, (2) you and your clients, and (3) you and your referral network.

Our firm's culture discourages the internal competitiveness or mistrust among lawyers that can inhibit cross-selling. We encourage our lawyers to take advantage of every opportunity to promote their fellow lawyers for the benefit of the firm as a whole. Most find this easier than promoting themselves. For example, while having breakfast with a client, one of our partners learned that his client's estate plan needed updating. Ever alert to new business opportunities, the attorney touted the tax planning expertise of a fellow partner. Immediately after breakfast, he introduced his client to that partner and the client agreed to have his estate plan updated. This cross-selling of services was possible because the partner trusted his colleague to provide his client with the highest quality legal advice and personal service. In this case, everybody wins. The firm acquires additional work and the client sees that the firm can meet more than just one of the client's legal needs.

Develop your clients' trust by showing that you are always looking out for their best interests. Pay attention to issues that affect your clients so that you can assist them before problems arise. This helps cement a relationship and may lead to more work.

For example, our work for one of our largest clients began with just one small matter. Historically another law firm handled all the company's land use work. Our lawyer kept current on new regulations affecting the company. At no charge to the client and without being asked, the lawyer attended a critical public meeting about these new regulations. He made certain that members of the company noted his presence by talking to them about the significance of the meeting. As a result, the company asked the lawyer to join their team to deal with these new developments. Our work for this client has since expanded to more than seventy matters and we now handle their land use work almost exclusively. We continue to earn their trust by monitoring and keeping them informed of the events that affect their industry.

Forming and maintaining a network of business relationships is also an important part of your marketing plan. To establish a good referral network, start with the people you know. Focus on the individuals within your peer group who are likely to become the future leaders in business and industry. It may take several years, but those relationships will eventually develop into productive referral sources. When your peers reach positions of leadership in which they need to purchase legal services or make referrals, they will want to turn to a lawyer they already know and trust. Be that lawyer!

The Eighteen-Hole
Satellite Office

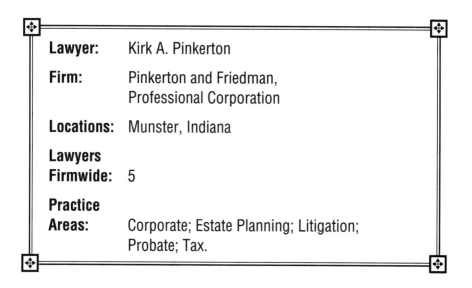

Lawyer: Kirk A. Pinkerton

Firm: Pinkerton and Friedman,
                Professional Corporation

Locations: Munster, Indiana

**Lawyers
Firmwide:**   5

**Practice
Areas:**   Corporate; Estate Planning; Litigation;
                Probate; Tax.

We are a small law firm in a relatively small community, so our marketing approach might be a little different from some larger firms. We have five lawyers. The largest firm in our area has thirty lawyers.

Our firm is regarded as a specialty or boutique firm. We do sophisticated estate planning, tax work, and transactional work. The type of work we do is what sets us apart from the other seven hundred lawyers in Lake County, Indiana. We do not represent any institutional clients, and we do not do any advertising.

Our marketing and practice development plan is not really organized or thought out because our work is all transactional and our clients do not generally require ongoing legal services. However, marketing is a priority for us and we are all constantly on the hunt for new business. We primarily market by being involved in the community and by joining local business clubs. We also put on seminars to discuss estate planning and pension issues, and we have participated in panel discussions for the State Bar of Indiana. Generally, this is the type of ongoing marketing that we do.

What one marketing technique has worked the best for me consistently over the years? I have one that I have used on an ongoing basis that has brought me more client work than anything else: golf. I have always loved to play golf, and I decided fifteen years ago that I should join the local country club and begin playing golf on a more regular basis so that I could meet people and develop business. I was soon elected to serve on the board of directors for the country club and was eventually elected president of the board. Fifteen years later, 25 to 30 percent of my clients have been generated as a result of my involvement in the country club.

I refer to the golf course as my "satellite office" and frequently run into my clients on the course.

From a small firm perspective, these client relationships are extremely important. We work hard to maintain these relationships and to develop new ones. We also try to ensure that our lawyers are involved in civic groups that will help facilitate relationships.

So, my greatest marketing "testimonial" is that being involved in the community really pays off. I would recommend this to any lawyer, not just lawyers who specialize in estate planning. Ours is a relationship business, so get out to the golf course or get involved in an activity that you enjoy. It provides a good way to meet people and develop new clients and referral sources for your firm.

More Than Just Credibility

Lawyer: Susan Raridon

Firm: Hildebrandt, Inc.

Locations: Somerville, New Jersey

Practice
Areas: Consulting to Law Firms

My experience has shown that there are two primary types of marketing activities for lawyers: credibility building and direct marketing. Most lawyers—by personality type, inclination, or interest—are not natural rainmakers. Thus, they must first undertake credibility-building activities to enhance their chances of attracting business. Credibility builders include speaking at seminars or conferences, writing articles, and receiving significant honors or appointments (such as an invitation into the American College of Trial Lawyers or the American College of Trusts and Estate Counsel).

Later, once you have developed a reputation as an expert in an area of law, you have a higher likelihood of success in your direct marketing activities. Direct marketing includes networking, client and prospect entertainment, formal and informal pitches, presentations or "beauty contests," and other personal contacts. This is the "selling" part with which many lawyers are still uncomfortable. One key is that if you have done sufficient credibility builders over the years, you often do not have to sell directly with your personal contact to get the business.

Every lawyer needs a balance of these two types of activities. Many of us become comfortable with the credibility activities, which are not "unseemly" or "unprofessional" like selling. We give several speeches or write several articles a year. Unfortunately, you reach a point of diminishing returns at which these activities are less important or successful. At that point, you should only do a few maintenance credibility builders each year or take them on for "defensive" reasons (e.g., if you do not accept the speaking slot at a conference, one of your competitors will). You then also need to shift most of your time to direct marketing activities.

I found this true in my consulting practice too. Giving ten or more speeches a year and writing several articles was important early in my career, but once I had established a substantial reputation, I found that the way to attract more business was primarily through direct marketing.

Advertising and Partnering

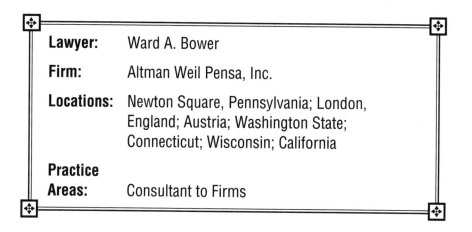

Lawyer: Ward A. Bower

Firm: Altman Weil Pensa, Inc.

Locations: Newton Square, Pennsylvania; London, England; Austria; Washington State; Connecticut; Wisconsin; California

Practice
Areas: Consultant to Firms

Although I consult to law firms rather than practice law, the marketing principles are the same. The theme "personal success in marketing" brings two examples to mind—one dealing with advertising and the other with "partnering" with clients by introducing them to opportunities they otherwise would not experience.

We ran an advertising campaign in the mid-1980s focusing on discrete, specialized services and individual Altman Weil Pensa consultants, designed to demonstrate our capabilities. One particular ad inspired a managing partner of a major law firm to call and say "I have your picture in front of me and I feel compelled to call you." The result was a client relationship that has extended almost a decade, involved multiple iterations of the strategic planning process, and generated hundreds of thousands of dollars in consulting fees.

The second example involved our assisting a United Kingdom firm to evaluate its international strategies, the result of which was an introduction to a United States law firm client seeking a London office. The U.K. firm represents British and Irish entertainers who work in the United States and need U.S. immigration, contract, and commercial representation; the U.S. firm represents corporations transferring American executives abroad and thus need immigration services in the United Kingdom and Europe. The result of our introduction was the opportunity to put together an early trans-Atlantic affiliation agreement, one of the first between a U.S. and a U.K. firm, and to position ourselves favorably with both clients for continued consulting representation. Additionally, the publicity resulting from the affiliation reflected favorably on our international consulting capabilities.

There is no reason why law firms cannot employ similar advertising, demonstrating expertise and credentials, in publications directed toward corporate counsel and also partner with clients by exposing them to outbound business and investment opportunities, with the ability to perform the coincidental legal work.

PART 2

Developing a Marketing Program: Ideas That Work

Avoiding the Worst Mistakes

Lawyer:	Mindy G. Farber
Firm:	Jacobs, Jacobs & Farber
Locations:	Rockville, Maryland
Lawyers Firmwide:	7
Practice Areas:	Employment and Labor Law; Professional Malpractice; Personal Injury; Product Liability; Business and Contract Law; Family Law; Corporations; Estate Planning, Wills, and Trust Law; Workers' Compensation Law; Criminal Law; General Civil and Criminal Trial and Appellate Practice in State and Federal Courts; Federal Regulatory and Administrative Law.

Six years ago I was a middle-level partner at a medium-sized law firm, enjoying what many would think to be an appreciably respectable salary but without any way to jimmy a rigid lockstep compensation system and truly soar to the top. As an employment and labor law lawyer, I was well aware six years ago that the practice was becoming hot, hot, hot, and that with a little bit of courage, making it on my own would be the best way to have my business flourish. I was tired of bloated overhead compressing my salary, and frankly, I was also tired of not being able to run a practice the way I wanted to, whether I ultimately won or lost, succeeded or failed. So, with two children under the age of six, I founded my own practice, begged my secretary to come with me (promising that even if I did not get paid, she would), and wondered what on earth I had done.

Six years later, I have a beautiful office, soon-to-be three associates, the same super secretary, and, most importantly, what I believe my colleagues view as a solid reputation in the same field of law, employment and labor, which is still hot, hot, hot.

In articles I have written, I have stressed what I have done to be successful. In this book, I think it is just as important to stress the mistakes I have avoided, which I see many lawyers, young and old, day after day, blunder into, much to their detriment. To that end, here is some advice.

UNLESS YOU ARE ALAN DERSHOWITZ, DON'T LOOK LIKE A SCHLEP

First, I want to tell you that I hate the dress-for-success look and always have. Second, I want to tell you that I was once a middle-class hippie with the correct work shirt, work boots, and ripped up jeans. What I am trying to say, I guess, is that I am not uptight. Still, I cannot emphasize enough how appearance in the '90s does matter. It never ceases to astonish me, when I give presentations on marketing and rainmaking, how bad many lawyers look. The same disheveled lawyers will take careful notes and give their most rapt attention to my marketing tips and techniques but think nothing of looking so terrible, which negates everything I have taught. If a client is going to shell out money, why would he or she want to pay for a lousy-looking lawyer? A lousy-looking lawyer promotes the notion of an unsuccessful lawyer. If you are unsuccessful, nobody wants to hire you. Furthermore, your biggest client—or any client—may unexpectedly walk in on you at any time, and you do not want to be embarrassed about how you look. If you follow the rule of thumb to look great all the time, you will get somewhere in your practice, I promise.

WORK YOUR YOU-KNOW-WHAT OFF

Unless you work your—okay, I'll say it—butt off, you are not going to succeed, and boy, do I work hard. I do not say this to give myself the proverbial pat on the back, but again, it simply astonishes me that some lawyers think that all they have to do is go to a seminar in marketing, take some copious notes, and expect that a lot of business will somehow flood through their doors. These same lawyers will switch their answering machines on at 5:00 p.m. and think that clients will somehow find them. They simply do not spend the vast amount of time necessary to generate business.

If you want to succeed, you have to work harder than you ever thought possible. You must write articles, read new case law, network with friends, and volunteer to do seminars. You need to think about how to bring in new business—and do the work to get it. When your family goes to bed at night, you need to do more work. On bleak Sunday nights, you need to do some work. The point is, it does not come easy to any of us, no matter how easy it sounds. Unless you are willing to commit the hours, you are not going to have a successful practice.

On the other hand, you may simply not want to work that hard. That is okay—just do not expect to build a big practice. You will stay small, and that is perfectly acceptable, if that is what *you* want.

NO ONE IN THE KNOW HANGS OUT
A SHINGLE NOWADAYS

Clearly the key to really doing well is specializing. Before you go into your own practice, look around you at the fields that are going strongly. The point is, you have to develop a reputation as an expert in a specialized field. It is not good enough to dabble, do a little bit of everything, and expect to create fireworks. Nowadays, there are thousands of lawyers everywhere and anywhere. There is absolutely no reason why business will come your way unless you have a gimmick. The gimmick in the practice of law is specializing. I picked up my specialty by doing civil rights work for the government before going into private practice. But my specialty grew even without that background. I have bought many books on my subject matter over time; I read all the developing case law; I put the word out to every other lawyer that I specialize; and I write and speak, speak and write.

The point of all this should be that when any other lawyer in your county or your city or your state gets a case that he or she cannot or does not want to do, he or she should immediately think of you as the specialist in that area and refer the case. The ultimate success is getting a referral from a lawyer you simply do not know. It is not going to happen, however, if you put out a shingle saying that you have a general practice. Obviously there are lawyer exceptions who have profited from a general practice, but not too many *nowadays*.

GOOD CLIENTS RESPOND TO RESPECTABLE FEES
AND RETAINERS, NOT FREEBIES AND DISCOUNTS

If you want good clients, you have to look like you know what you are doing. If you know what you are doing, you will charge respectable rates and respectable retainers. Overall, you do not get good clients by discounting heavily or offering cut-rate prices. Cut-rate prices merely reflect a lawyer who is not doing well and does not feel comfortable competing. Therefore, take a deep breath, take a gamble, and charge an absolutely respectable retainer and forthright hourly rate. It is an absolute fallacy to think that you are going to attract clients by conducting your own personal price war. It just does not work in the practice of law. I have had many experiences where clients talked to me and then to another lawyer at a lower rate. They have invariably chosen to come to me because they figure I know what I am talking about, given the self-confidence I have in establishing my rates. Simply, if you act cheap and look cheap, you are going to get clients who are cheap—and that is not enough to pay your bills.

The point is that you have to be self-confident and, more importantly, *act* and *appear* self-confident. The key to a successful practice is looking like you know what you are doing. The alternative? A third-rate office charging third-rate prices facing a third-rate future. The biggest mistake of them all.

Ten Minutes a Day to Marketing Success

Lawyer:	Donna M. Killoughey
Firm:	Law Offices of Donna M. Killoughey
Locations:	Tempe, Arizona
Lawyers Firmwide:	1
Practice Areas:	Bankruptcy; Commercial Products Liability; Landlord-Tenant; Probate and Wills; Personal Injury.

A book of business does not appear overnight. It results from years of developing relationships with professional peers, personal friends, and community and business acquaintances. Because it can take years for one contact to produce a "return," there must be frequent reminders to your contacts of where you are and what you are doing. In the minds and attitudes of clients and client senders, you must first be remembered; then you must be viewed as one who can be trusted, who is thorough, competent, up-to-date, and responsive.

Ongoing communication is essential to development of a business relationship. The requisite level of communication to initiate a circle of clients takes no more than ten minutes a day.

The daily checklist presented here is intended to motivate and assist lawyers who have never marketed themselves as well as those who have very little time available for the development of personal marketing skills. The premise is that "once you begin, the rest is easy." From a psychological point of view, each individual lawyer should do something in the way of personal marketing every day for at least twenty-one days (including weekends), after which time the skills may become automatic, or at least more comfortable.

By using the checklist daily, you will get in the habit of planning and following through with marketing activities. Results should begin to occur only after a few months of continuous activity. Of course, further relationship building (which is the foundation of personal marketing success) takes more time than ten minutes per day. However, part of your personal marketing plan should be to develop clients for others in the office to work on, so that your time is later freed up to spend much more than the daily ten minutes on the more time-consuming aspects of marketing.

MARKETING CHECKLIST

1. General Activities
   — Write down your plan
   — Make lists of
   - Clients you enjoy
   - Practice areas you enjoy
   - Your target clients
   - Your target practice areas
   - Who you know, including your close friends
   - Who your employees know
   — Plan your marketing activities for the month, week, and day
   — Send a general business letter to
   - Someone you met within the last week
   - A social acquaintance
   - A continuing legal education contact
   - Alumni in another state
   — Send personal notes of congratulations regarding
   - An election, appointment, or promotion
   - A case result
   - A personal event, such as a wedding, birthday, or business expansion
   - A book or article publication
   - A name in print
   — Make two calls to set up a networking meeting with
   - Another lawyer
   - A doctor
   - An accountant
   - Another businessperson
   — Call clients you have not spoken with in a while

(continued)

— Read a non-law publication for
  • New leads or business opportunities
  • Interesting marketing ideas
— Read the *Directory of Associations* to learn
  • Which you can join
  • Who you know in a given association
— Read the Yellow Pages to find out
  • Who the specialists in your field are (and contact them for referrals)
  • What businesses you want as clients (and make a list)
— Read the lists you make and *use them*
— Obtain the mailing list for group(s) in which you participate
— Study your client base, work performance, and results, including
  • Fees billed and collected per area
  • Fees per client
  • Sources of referrals
— Load up your car, daytime organizer, purse, wallet, and pocket with business development materials, including
  • Business cards
  • Thank-you note cards
  • Memo sheets for handwritten notes
  • Greeting cards
— Collect business cards at meetings and
  • Add them to your database
  • Write notes on the reverse side about where and when you met the person

(continued)

- File hard copies in your marketing binder
- Follow up on these as you run out of other leads
— Take a consultant or rainmaker to lunch and ask how they do it and what you can do for your client development
— Develop form letters, including
  - "Thank you for the referral of . . ."
  - "I have referred _____ to you. Please give special attention if they call."
— Update your résumé, and give it a fresh look
— Create portions of a "Summary of Professional Achievements" that tells what you have done (*not* where you have been), including
  - Cases you have tried, settled, and arbitrated (but be aware of confidentiality)
  - Ongoing client matters (generically described)
  - Courts in which you have appeared
  - Transactions you have completed
  - Management and financial experience in volunteer or professional organizations
2. Substantive Activities
   — Fill out an application for membership in an organization related to your area of interest, such as
     - American Bankruptcy Institute
     - Credit Union Attorneys organizations
     - U.S. Trustee Association
     - National Association of Female Executives
   — Read *Martindale-Hubbell* to identify practitioners with a different client base who are not likely to do your work

(*continued*)

— Define how your practice is expanding, and write it down
— Contact friends in larger or noncompeting practice areas and firms and
   • Ask them to send small cases or conflicts
   • Ask what you can send them and why you should

Inexpensive Marketing for the Solo Lawyer

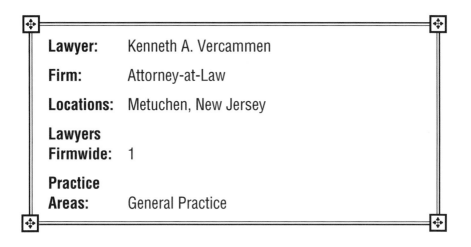

Lawyer:	Kenneth A. Vercammen
Firm:	Attorney-at-Law
Locations:	Metuchen, New Jersey
Lawyers Firmwide:	1
Practice Areas:	General Practice

My law office is on a main street in a close-knit town in the metropolitan New York area, nineteen miles north of Princeton. The following ideas are ones that I have found effective in a suburban or rural community. No business, whether it is a large law firm, a solo practice, or even a pizza shop, will stay in business unless it can continue to bring in business and adapt to the times. We all need to conduct activities that will promote a positive image of the legal profession as well as enable us to generate sufficient income to pay our bills. Client relations and marketing often consist merely of being nice to people—our clients, the mail carrier, our neighbors, and strangers. In this book, I would like to share a few simple, low-cost, and effective ideas on personal marketing.

HOW TO WIN FRIENDS AND INFLUENCE PEOPLE

Dale Carnegie wrote many books and gave many lectures on the theme of his most famous publication, How to Win Friends and Influence People. I purchased his hardcover book and also bought the audiotapes of the book to listen to in my car. At least once a year I read the book or listen to the tapes to remind me to think positive and be nice to people. When my office sent out a client survey to all clients, I was pleasantly surprised that many of them responded with comments that they felt we cared about them as people and did not simply view our clients as a method of making money.

GREAT CHINESE FOOD!

The small businesses and other non-chains in the suburbs are struggling against the big malls and the franchises. When I receive good service, or great food at a local restaurant, I send the owner or manager a letter of thanks on my law office letterhead. This makes these owners feel good, and they give priority service to me and my wife when we return. Several stores even framed my letter and hung it up for their customers to see. Thank-you letters are inexpensive and provide great goodwill for the legal profession.

HOLIDAY PARTY GOODWILL

Back in high school and college, I organized parties to meet girls and later to become a "big man on campus." On the advice of marketing expert and lawyer Susan Raridon, beginning in 1987 I began organizing social affairs for charity groups. We charged only five to ten dollars per person and arranged with a nightclub to provide a complimentary hot and cold buffet. Since 1987 thousands of young professionals have attended these charity socials and it has generated friends for me and lots of publicity for the charity groups.

With increased visibility thanks to a growing personal injury and litigation practice, I was selected as a cochair for the Seventh Annual Christmas Brew Ho-Ho. This annual party is sponsored by a variety of professional groups, including the New Jersey Bar, the Society of Young CPAs, and the State Chiropractic Society. We raised substantial money at the Brew Ho-Ho for the Make a Wish Foundation. Between our five cosponsors, we mailed ten thousand full-page flyers. This generated goodwill for the bar association, plus goodwill for the cochair and me, who were listed on the flyers.

FREE WATER

Many towns across the country, including mine, host community fairs and carnivals. Many nonprofit and ethnic groups usually sell baked goods, burgers, perogies, kielbasas, and a variety of ethnic foods at these events.

Our law office regularly sets up a table to provide free spring water. "Free" is a big attraction to people, and many people with health concerns cannot drink soda or other sweetened beverages. Our table also has free legal and consumer booklets authored by members of our firm on topics including wills, real estate, living wills, probate, and personal injury. The senior citizens love the free material and we have become one of the most popular booths. This technique is very successful, and we hope to continue to serve the community at upcoming town events, including providing hot chocolate at the Christmas parade and spring water at the Spring Festival and Memorial Day Parade.

ESTATE PLANNING SEMINARS

While I do not practice tax law, our firm is organizing an estate planning and tax seminar to help the middle class cope with the largest budget tax increase in history. The program is set up to feature three speakers: an energetic CPA, a vice president of Dean Witter (the stockbrokers and investment counselors), and me. I am sending invitations to three thousand friends, clients, relatives, and professionals.

Our programs for consumers are always free to the public. We supply soda, cookies, cakes, and complimentary consumer materials. We ask that each attendee donate a can of food to the Community Food Bank of New Jersey.

If you are going to speak publicly to a group, I suggest that you practice your talk on a tape recorder several times before your speech. By reviewing your talk, you can improve content and streamline your presentation.

NEIGHBORHOOD PICNICS AND NEWSLETTERS

A few years ago, I served as a Town Democratic Committeeperson in an area of approximately eight hundred voters. Each year of my term, I invited everyone to my backyard to play volleyball and horseshoes, eat burgers, and meet elected officials. My wife and I now combine the party with my son's birthday party. This small gathering promotes goodwill among our neighbors.

My wife and I also publish a neighborhood newsletter. We inform people in the neighborhood about (1) accomplishments that improve our town (e.g., painting of park swings); (2) upcoming nonprofit events (e.g., the Edison Elks Fish Fry, Knights of Columbus Octoberfest, Lunch with Santa); and (3) general legal topics that will interest local citizens (e.g., car insurance laws, car lemon laws, divorce laws). We use desktop publishing on the easy-to-use Macintosh computer. For less than two hundred dollars, we have five hundred four-page newsletters printed.

During my morning jog, I run house to house dropping off the neighborhood newsletter to local homes. We have received great feedback, and we have obtained many clients from this effort.

SOLO'S OFFICE BROCHURE

Many large law firms have sent me their expensive, glossy firm brochures. For solos and small firms, full-color printed brochures are a waste of money. To create a low-cost brochure, my office uses our photocopier. Our firm brochure begins in paragraph form discussing the firm's practice, then trial and litigation experience. We also include a revised copy of my legal résumé, legal publication list, legal seminars attended, list of community involvement activities, prepaid legal plan participation, and speakers bureau activities. All pages are reduced in size to fit two pages on one side of a sheet of legal paper. The brochure is then photocopied on three legal-size sheets, front and back, and then folded over for a great twelve-page brochure. My experience and background on paper impresses new clients who initially wonder whether a young solo lawyer has the experience to help them. All clients are impressed by my continued legal education and publication list.

One last marketing suggestion: To learn more about marketing and office efficiency, join both the ABA's Law Practice Management Section and General Practice Section.

The WINIT Program

Lawyer: Robert M. Beck Jr.

Firm: Stites & Harbison

Locations: Lexington, Kentucky; Louisville, Kentucky; Frankfort, Kentucky; Jeffersonville, Kentucky

Lawyers Firmwide: Over 100

Practice Areas: General Civil Practice in All State and Federal Courts; Acquisitions, Divestitures, and Mergers; Administrative Hearings and Appeals; Admiralty; Antitrust; Appellate Practice; Aviation; Banking; Bankruptcy; Charitable Trusts and Foundations; Commercial; Complex Litigation; Construction; Corporation; Defense of Legal and Medical Malpractice and Personal Injury; Dissolution of Marriage; Employment; Environmental; Equine; Estate Planning and Probate Administration; Health Care; Insurance Defense; Labor; Legislative Practice; Litigation; Mineral; Planning and Zoning; Public Finance; Products Liability Litigation; Real Estate; Securities; Social Security Disability; Local, State, Federal, Estate, and Gift Taxation; Toxic Torts Litigation; Trusts; Utilities.

Most lawyers realize that the cornerstone of marketing is providing quality legal work. We are all in competition with firms that provide quality service to clients on an ongoing basis. The key is to provide the best service possible by listening to your clients, identifying their needs and desires, and asking them questions to determine their goals and their desired end results.

Our firm started a program a few years ago that has helped our lawyers to develop the attitude that we are partners with our clients. The program is titled WINIT (for "We're In It Together"), and it is a total quality management (TQM) program for client service. The basic premise is that you have to listen to what the clients want and provide them with the type of service that they need within the cost and time parameters that are established. The WINIT program is one method we have used to differentiate our firm from other law firms. It is based on our "Ten Imperatives of Client Service."

1. Be accessible.
2. Be reliable.
3. Be responsive.
4. Provide assurance.
5. Show empathy.
6. Pay attention to tangibles.
7. Communicate.
8. Show initiative.
9. Add value.
10. Recover from service errors.

By establishing these ten imperatives, our firm has sensitized people to the needs of our clients. The WINIT program was initiated with a half-day firmwide "pep rally," which included all lawyers and staff. We all loaded into buses, hired temps to cover our switchboard, and convened off-site to learn the value of working closer as a team. Our lawyers and staff have responded very well to the program. Although the program is multifaceted, it is basically a marketing initiative.

Our clients have noticed a change in the way we do business, and they perceive the WINIT program as a joint effort that includes them. We have truly created a marketing program to which our clients respond positively.

We generate new ideas about how to improve our level of service under the WINIT program on an ongoing basis. We recently formed a WINIT subcommittee to identify new tools that will enable our lawyers to solicit feedback from our clients. We added language to our standard engagement letter to make it more "client oriented." The standard letter now includes information on timeliness of delivery, how quickly we will return phone calls, what type of communication the client will receive in writing on a regular basis (e.g., does the client want copies of all pleadings or just certain ones), and other matters. I believe that the clients appreciate the development of these expectations at the beginning of the engagement. We make every attempt to satisfy their requests.

The subcommittee also developed a program to insert sets of postcards into bills sent to clients. These are small cards that ask how we are doing. This is a fairly new program, so we have not yet been able to judge its success, but we are hopeful that it will provide clients with a vehicle to voice their opinions about our service.

As part of my service, I like to learn as much as possible about my clients' businesses. I routinely go to their places of business and see how they operate. I take a real interest in their success. I do it on my free time and often provide free advice regarding issues that I perceive need to be addressed. I like to have the opportunity to create value or synergy for clients. In that vein, I will provide a personal example of a successful marketing effort using the WINIT approach.

I am active in the equine industry. Lexington is the capital of the thoroughbred breeding industry. I am an avid reader of information that I believe may affect my clients. In 1988, I was reading the ABA *Journal* and found out about a new United Nations Convention on the International Sale of Goods. As I was reading the article, I realized that this issue would have some impact on my clients who were engaged in equine transactions internationally. There was not much existing case law, so I began researching the subject and created an in-depth paper on the convention. I was a featured speaker at a seminar and gave a presentation on this topic, and, immediately following the seminar, an individual came up to me and said he needed help with this very issue. He was selling a horse from the United States to Japanese customers and needed some advice. I was immediately hired as his lawyer and have, over the years, developed considerable expertise on this subject.

I believe my success in this area is attributable to, first, reading articles that have impact on my clients; second, having the vision to learn more about specific areas of practice; and third, marketing myself in this area. It took vision and a lot of work to develop an understanding of the law, but it led directly and immediately to business, which in turn, led directly to expertise and a reputation in this area.

Everybody Can Make Rain!

Lawyer:	Donna D. Fraiche
Firm:	Locke Purnell Rain Harrell
Locations:	New Orleans, Louisiana; Dallas, Texas; Austin, Texas
Lawyers Firmwide:	Over 200
Practice Areas:	Full-Service Law Firm

I have used a wide variety of rainmaking approaches in my own practice and in advising and mentoring others. I would like to share my marketing experiences gained from a twenty-one-year history in the practice of law, which includes practicing in a variety of different settings. This history has greatly affected my appreciation of the value of client service. I presently have a national practice in the area of health care. I previously was a named partner in a firm that I helped to form and now am with a very large traditional law firm. In this book, I would like to share and compare the experiences.

In a newly organized firm, rainmaking is essential as the blood and lifeline of the firm. I never had an institutional base of clients offered to me as part of a firm setting, so I had to create my own. My basic rainmaking philosophy is to identify with the client by recognizing the client's needs. I believe this gives me an advantage, since most institutional firms promote what might be good for the firm in the short term rather than what is good for the client in the long term. It is important to make sure that the *client's* needs are met. Traditional marketing notions include such activities as educational outreach, speech making, and communicating developments in a particular industry, or the legal and regulatory changes that affect that particular client and its industry. This philosophy has served me well over the years. There are a number of examples of how total client service equates to successful rainmaking, including the following.

Know your practice area well.   By undertaking to develop knowledge and skills in a particular practice area, you gain the ability to speak your client's language. By the same token, clients will come to identify you with the regulatory or other changes that you have freely shared with them as a value-added service to your relationship. Clients are not charged for this service. It is simply part of the advantage of being associated with someone who cares about their business and their interests.

Be in the right place at the right time.   So very much of getting clients on the front end is luck—being at the right meetings, or being available when the phone rings and a potential client is on the other end. Yet you can enhance your odds if you have certain simple practices that are part of your individual culture. It can be as simple as having a very quick response time to telephone calls, perhaps by having administrative staff who are very sensitive to getting in touch with you and getting back to clients within a short time of when they call.

Involve everyone. Clients need to know that you are in touch with them and their situation as well as your own office at all times. This is an *internal* approach to rainmaking that puts at issue the internal environment of the firm so that everyone participates in client service, including the receptionist, librarians, paralegals, associates, legal secretaries, and administrators.

Develop an external approach. Service on community boards can help in developing an *external* reputation as a leader. In situations where potential clients can learn of a lawyer's articulation or other communication skills, the ground is fertile for development of credibility, trustworthiness, and know-how. However, it should be cautioned that service on boards and respective committees of boards can be extremely time-consuming and should not be undertaken if there is not the time capacity to do so and to do so well. I prepare for board and committee meetings as I would for any other professional undertaking. I only serve on boards where relevant issues are discussed in a way that I can make a meaningful contribution. The "good old boy" networks thrive on interpersonal board relationships, and as a woman I have found similar opportunities for stimulating discussion and professional interaction.

Professional reputation is critical. Lawyers are spokespersons for their clients in different settings. In and out of the courtroom, in and out of the negotiation room, and in and out of the office, lawyers are looked upon for their communication skills. Developing a reputation as a quotable expert in a given arena will allow a potential rainmaker tremendous positive exposure. If a new development occurs, be prepared to give a sixty-second statement on the subject. Be quotable. Be able to speak to issues relative to your practice area in a commonsense way. Do not "overlawyerize" a particular subject so as to confuse your audience.

Expose your clients to other helpful contacts and opportunities to meet and network.   Clients, potential clients, and referral sources can gain much from knowing each other and sharing or networking resource opportunities.

Have a keen business sense.   Clients have budgetary needs and requirements. Clients will no longer write blank checks to lawyers. The careful rainmaker will communicate up front the potential cost of undertaking a project. A new client that a rainmaker worked very hard to get can be easily lost if the first bill presents a proverbial goose that laid a golden egg. Review with your clients how much of your service may be required and how their bills will be formatted, when they will be sent, and what your payment expectations are. Help your clients plan to use the resources you make available to them.

Work as a team.   Do not pretend to be the expert when someone else may be more qualified. Find the best people to fulfill your clients' needs—whether those people are in your firm or not—and access those resources by introducing them to your clients. Cross-sell the other members of your firm, as it is much easier to speak highly of their capabilities than of your own. I treat clients I bring to the firm as *clients of the firm*. I feel personally responsible for providing the highest level of service to clients through supervising and monitoring their matters at different levels and through different teams within the firm. There have even been times when I have had to recommend strongly that we seek a particular service outside of the firm to meet the client's needs. A cost-effective and quality team approach is a desirable way to handle a client's important business.

Rainmaking is a time-consuming and massive undertaking. Individual professionals must look honestly at their highest and best use. Are they better externally, spending their time getting business? Are they better providing quality service internally? Are they better at handling client retention issues and keeping the client pleased for the long term? Lawyers must be honest with themselves, and although everyone has the capability to make rain, not everyone can make rain in the same way.

Balance your quality of life. Rainmakers have a schizophrenic lifestyle. They are constantly pulled and tugged in a variety of directions, including origination, direct client service, administrative and billing responsibilities, continuing professional education, giving speeches, writing articles, keeping in touch with clients' birthdays and anniversaries, and finally, somewhere in the midst, the most important priorities, family and friends. The tension that exists among competing responsibilities can be balanced if the rainmaker is sensitive to personal approaches in developing business. Where professionally appropriate, clients can be invited to participate in dinner meetings including family members. Telephone conferences can be scheduled from cottage-based settings, such as ski trips and family vacations (although I would not advise doing this frequently, given the family dynamic). Rainmakers have to make sacrifices like eighteen holes of golf when nine would do just as well. Lastly, individuals have to make choices that are comfortable for them in combining a client service lifestyle with competing interests within time constraints.

Increased competition produces creative results. There are more lawyers with fewer work opportunities to go around. In-house counsel are sophisticated about the kind of legal service they require in that they want to pay for it.

Rainmakers must be sensitive to creative approaches in bringing in new clients and retaining the existing ones.

Track headlines for your clients. Daily newspapers can provide a plethora of opportunities by way of new issues and information important to a client or potential client who simply does not have time to thumb through every publication and current events periodical that passes his or her desk. For example, an information gold mine could include the filings, zoning board hearings, late-breaking bankruptcy filings, and causes of action that may trigger interest and response on the part of clients and potential clients. The fast-track approach toward disseminating new information demonstrates a level of awareness and concern about a client. It says to a client, "I saw this article and immediately thought of you. What do you think?" If a new case is decided on a subject relevant to a particular client, copy the case and attach a bullet-pointed and simplistic summary of the development and how it might affect that client's business and needs. These sensitive approaches toward dissemination of information can be undertaken by anyone in the organization who, with an eagle eye, is trained to be always on the lookout for the client's needs. I have the receptionist in my office scan the daily newspapers to clip all articles concerning health care developments. Many of these articles find their way into my clients' offices through their fax machines, with my name identified in the context of thinking of their needs.

Maintain a geographic database. In addition to the standard alphabetical format, I record contact information according to geographic destination. If I meet someone from a city in the northeast who may be a referral counsel or source of business, his or her name is kept in a geographic database so that when trips are planned to that region I can fit in as many breakfasts, lunches, and dinners as possible to create the most meetings and contacts out of one particular trip. These contacts are repeated over a series of time, and credible friendships and professional relationships are formed for the long term. I always follow up these meetings with a note that references a tidbit of the discussion we shared as well as personal information to personalize the memory of the meeting. I always invite the contacts to visit on their next trip to my city.

Develop unhackneyed networks. Everyone has a network that presents a development opportunity. Networks can include professional associations, friendships, even family members. A network member may be valuable to other members of your firm. As discussed earlier, it is a lot easier to introduce the attributes of a coworker than to applaud your own. In a network context, it could be very easy for you to think of ten professionals in your community that you would like to get to know better. You may wish to host a dinner where you are the only person who knows everyone there and have everyone go around the room and introduce themselves, their businesses, and the opportunities and events in their lives that may be of interest to the group.

Spend money on marketing. Most major corporations in this country effectively budget for image making and design. They are serious about the way they look, their public relations, and how they are perceived in their market. Lawyers traditionally have shied away from advertising. However, the more subtle forms of marketing, which have been professionally condoned, can be effective if well presented, thought out, and bought. Firms spend money buying tables at charity balls to get exposure in a positive way in the community. This may or may not be effective, but it is one way that the firm can put its name out. Buying lunches and dinners for clients can become cost prohibitive if such occasions do not result in meaningful fee-based production. Using resources such as holiday greetings and announcements can be expensive given the cost of printing and postage, but it can be effective if even one such card lands on the desk of a prospective client. At the end of the day it is important to weigh the benefits versus the costs.

There are no fixed rules. All of these points of reference have been used directly and indirectly in my own practice over the past twenty-one years. Some techniques have been more successful than others, but all of these techniques must be natural and unforced to be effective. The final successful point that I want to relate is simply sharing successful rainmaking techniques with others. Oddly enough, this activity, more than any other, has resulted in the production of new and lasting clients, referral counsel, and long-term relationships and friendships.

The 110 Percent Commitment

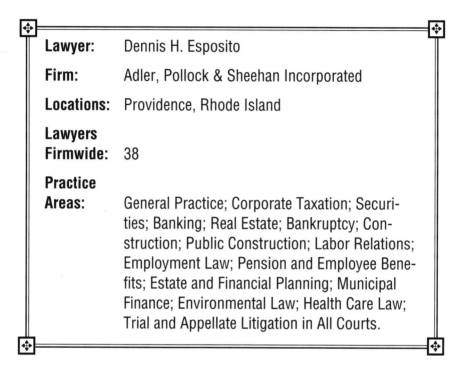

Lawyer: Dennis H. Esposito

Firm: Adler, Pollock & Sheehan Incorporated

Locations: Providence, Rhode Island

Lawyers Firmwide: 38

Practice Areas: General Practice; Corporate Taxation; Securities; Banking; Real Estate; Bankruptcy; Construction; Public Construction; Labor Relations; Employment Law; Pension and Employee Benefits; Estate and Financial Planning; Municipal Finance; Environmental Law; Health Care Law; Trial and Appellate Litigation in All Courts.

Effective marketing covers a broad spectrum of activities. Personally, I believe you can, and should, never stop marketing. It takes a "110 percent commitment," to use the hackneyed expression. You cannot sit back and wait for business to come to you. My personal philosophy centers around "proactive representation," or partnering with the client. While you need to understand what you perceive are the needs of the client, you must also understand what the client perceives those needs to be. You need to understand the client's business climate and how that climate affects the client's business. Once you grasp the "Total Client," incorporate this knowledge into everything you do for, or with, that client, or, if you or your firm has targeted the client's industry, with that industry as well. Take a proactive view of your practice and go after more business based on your specialized knowledge in that field.

The key here is "Total Client" knowledge and the key word is "proactive." You must use your specialized knowledge to keep your clients proactive—and to help them avoid waiting for things to happen to them. This will differentiate you from others in your field. Once you develop commitment, I suggest the following step-by-step approach:

1. Always deliver good work. You have to have the underlying skills to be a success, but remember that delivery is important, too.
2. Go out and tell people what you know. Through public speaking, writing, participation in seminars, and community involvement, share your thoughts and expertise. Focus on high-visibility activities.
3. Look for referrals. Often you can go to a recognized person in your field of expertise and ask for the names of four or five referral sources.
4. Don't forget your roots. Always send thank-you notes and ask clients how they were referred to you.
5. Get in their minds. Position yourself in the minds of industry contacts. They need to hear your name over and over again.

An Institutional Approach

```
┌─────────────────────────────────────────────┐
│ Lawyer:      Andrew M. Kramer                 │
│                                               │
│ Firm:        Jones, Day, Reavis & Pogue       │
│                                               │
│ Locations:   Columbus, Ohio; Cleveland, Ohio; Atlanta, Geor- │
│              gia; Brussels, Belgium; Chicago, Illinois; Dallas, │
│              Texas; Frankfurt, Germany; Geneva, Switzerland; │
│              Hong Kong; Irvine, California; London, England; │
│              Los Angeles, California; New York, New York; │
│              Paris, France; Pittsburgh, Pennsylvania; Riyadh, │
│              Saudi Arabia; Taipei, Taiwan; Tokyo, Japan; │
│              Washington, D.C.                 │
│                                               │
│ Lawyers                                       │
│ Firmwide:    Over 1,000                       │
│                                               │
│ Practicer                                     │
│ Areas:       Full-Service Law Firm            │
└─────────────────────────────────────────────┘
```

Being part of a large firm requires us to allocate client development resources on a fairly wide scale. At our firm we do a lot of things to attract new clients and enhance client relationships. Much of it is now institutionalized. In a short story like this, I cannot share all our techniques with the readers, but I can focus on a few programs that have become institutional programs in our firm because they work.

The first thing that comes to mind is that, traditionally, lawyers seldom take the time to meet with other lawyers in their firm who are responsible for significant clients. We make it a point to try to help individual lawyers in our firm analyze the work that we have done for significant clients. Every lawyer who manages a client relationship needs to be aware of things like: How many new matters have we opened for this client during the past year? How well are we doing with this client? What work are they giving us? Who else are they using? In today's changing legal environment, much of any lawyer's practice is commodity based. Clients can select from other firms to accomplish their goals. Thus, to enhance and build on client relationships effectively, lawyers have to understand fully what the client's needs are and how well those needs are being served.

At least once yearly we ask each billing lawyer in our firm to meet with clients and review all of the critical aspects of the relationship. This is part of a process that makes lawyers understand that they are accountable for client relationships. Unless there is a sense of this responsibility, it is difficult to expand, yet alone maintain, effective client relationships.

Setting standards for individual lawyer marketing objectives is an important concept for firms to adopt. Every firm, whether large or small, needs to impose some client relationship standards to give lawyers an indication of what is expected of them. Examples from our firm include the following:

1. Lawyers must meet with clients annually to discuss performance.
2. Each lawyer must identify at least two new areas of practice to talk about with his or her clients. Then that lawyer must set up meetings to introduce additional people in our firm to those clients. This facili-

tates two-way communication within the firm—lawyers must communicate with each other to learn what skills other lawyers in the firm can offer clients—and it also facilitates two-way communication with clients—it takes knowledge of the client to establish what additional services the client may need.

To facilitate follow-through of these standards, each of our offices has a partner who is responsible for client development activities. These partners check to ensure that follow-up takes place. To avoid creating too much paper, which will become lost on the lawyer's desk, we have a simple system whereby each of these client development lawyers simply walks down the hall on a regular basis to see how things are progressing. Then we have a monthly conference call between the client development lawyers in each office to talk about how we are doing.

Training our lawyers in the area of client service is something that is important to this firm. We have formal training programs three times a year, which last two and one-half days. These sessions cover every aspect of client services and we limit the sessions to a maximum of twelve individuals. This has enabled our firm to bring a considerable number of lawyers into the client development process.

Over the past few years, we have developed data on how our clients use our services. We look at how many new matters we open for these clients per year, and we analyze how integrated our work for a given client is on both an office and practice group basis.

One story comes to mind here. In one particular client situation, our relationship with the client was declining because of simple neglect. This had been a very good client, but we noticed in our regular client analysis that revenues were declining. The number-one priority in a situation like this is *not* to ignore it. We did an analysis of who was servicing this client and investigated the possibility of assigning new lawyers to take over service to this client. This was obviously a very sensitive and difficult thing to have to go through. We knew if we did not make immediate personnel changes we would lose the client. So we were proactive and changed the client relationships, and now this client is one of the top clients in our firm. We let the client know that we cared by assigning the right service team for its needs.

The key is to recognize the need to become proactive and develop programs that focus on client opportunities.

Marketing Success on
the Internet

Lawyer:	Lewis Rose
Firm:	Arent Fox Kintner Plotkin & Kahn
Locations:	Washington, D.C.; Bethesda, Maryland; Vienna, Virginia; New York, New York; Budapest, Hungary; Jeddah, Saudi Arabia
Lawyers Firmwide:	Over 200
Practice Areas:	General Practice; Agriculture; Antitrust and Trade Regulation; Banking; Bankruptcy; Communications; Corporate and Securities; Employee Benefit Plans; Energy; Environment; Food and Drug; Government Contracts; Health; Immigration; Intellectual Property; International; Labor; Legislation; Litigation; Real Estate and Tax Law; Sports and Entertainment Law; White-Collar Criminal.

I began developing more of an interest in computers and the Internet in August 1994, coinciding with the major league baseball strike. I am an avid baseball fan and found myself with some free time, so I discovered the World Wide Web. I began exchanging electronic mail with people, then created a biography for myself with hyperlinks to more-detailed information about my law practice.

I titled my Web home page "Advertising Law Internet Site," marked up about fifteen articles I had written and included those, then added materials the FTC sent to me on advertising law for consumers, and I was in business. In September 1994, the home page averaged 488 visitors a month. By January 1996, it averaged 11,000 visitors a month. I attributed this to two reasons: (1) I had added more information to our site, and (2) more people have access to the Internet.

I receive many e-mail messages from people with questions. Many are students wanting to write papers, some are consumers who have been ripped off, and some are prospective clients. On average I respond to between ten and twenty inquiries per week. If I do not have a conflict, I generally answer the inquiry. I find that about one out of ten of these inquiries comes from a potential client—a real prospect, ranging from Fortune 500 companies to start-up operations. The next question is, Can they afford me? I am with a large Washington, D.C., law firm and our rates are comparable to other large firms in this marketplace.

Overall, I have generated fifteen to twenty clients off the Web, most of these in the second half of 1995.

These relationships start out like any other, with a relatively small project initially. I communicate with my clients by e-mail all over the country. It takes time to develop a level of trust and an ongoing relationship with these clients—just like any other.

The key to my success on the Internet is due to my providing information that goes beyond traditional marketing fluff and my being dedicated enough to follow through on inquiries. I now do a considerable amount of speaking, writing, and responding to media inquiries. Through this exposure, I believe that I will derive long-term results from my Internet presence.

Corporate Representation Service—An Affordable Technique

```
┌─────────────────────────────────────────────┐
│ Lawyer:      Mark A. Robertson                │
│ Firm:        Robertson & Williams             │
│ Locations:   Oklahoma City, Oklahoma          │
│ Lawyers                                       │
│ Firmwide:    4                                │
│ Practice                                      │
│ Areas:       General Civil Practice; Trial and Appellate │
│              Practice in All State and Federal Courts; Corpo- │
│              rate; Securities; Franchising; Estate Planning; │
│              Probate; Aviation; Banking; Bankruptcy; Com- │
│              munications; Real Estate; Commercial; Enter- │
│              tainment; Oil and Gas Law; International Trusts. │
└─────────────────────────────────────────────┘
```

Our firm has an extensive corporate practice in which we represent many small and medium-sized businesses. Our services include advice on structuring business, incorporation documentation, contract and employment work, mergers, acquisitions, real estate matters, dissolutions, and other general corporate work. Several years ago we came up with a successful marketing technique known as the "Corporate Representation Service." Once yearly we send our corporate clients a bill for one hundred dollars and a questionnaire for them to complete that will enable us to determine what should go into the client's annual minutes.

We created a simple database to support the data for each corporation, including basic information such as names of officers, directors, and the like. Each year we have continued with this template, and we now use a number of substantive systems for performing the Corporate Representation Service, in which we prepare not only annual meeting minutes but also act as a service agent for clients, do corporate compliance checks, and prepare special meeting minutes for clients—all for only one hundred dollars per year. We have had a substantive system in place for ten years that generates the correspondence, reminders, minutes, and questionnaires, so in most instances, it requires ten to fifteen minutes of a lawyer's time per corporation per year to keep minutes up to date for small corporations. Some corporations may require several hours of lawyer time to prepare their minutes, but on the average, spread out over several hundred corporations, the work is still quite profitable—and yet a bargain for the clients.

It is a great service for our corporate clients. Moreover, the firm is able to use this pricing strategy to attract new clients in addition to generating significant additional work as a result of the audit questionnaires, which often uncover additional legal needs of corporate and individual clients. By using this substantive system to do corporate minutes, the firm is able to organize its corporate work better while marketing additional services.

Don't Forget "Internal" Marketing

Lawyer: Karen Estelle Carey

Firm: Womble Carlyle Sandridge & Rice, PLLC

Locations: Winston-Salem, North Carolina; Charlotte, North Carolina; Raleigh, North Carolina; Atlanta, Georgia

Lawyers
Firmwide: Over 100

Practice
Areas: General Civil Trial and Appellate Practice; Taxation; Corporation; Mergers and Acquisitions; Securities; Intellectual Property; Technology Licensing; Computer Law; Labor and Employment Discrimination; Bankruptcy; Negligence; Products Liability; Administrative; Civil Rights; Municipal Bonds and Financing; Aviation; Construction; Antitrust; Estate Planning; Probate; Trust; Real Estate; Insurance; Banking; Commercial; Environmental; Municipal; Health Care; International Business; Employee Retirement Plans; Family Law; Investment Law.

How can a large law firm maintain a unified sense of purpose and esprit de corps when it has a diverse client base and offices in several cities?

81

As one of the largest law firms in the Southeast with offices in Atlanta, Charlotte, Raleigh, and Winston-Salem, Womble Carlyle enjoys an advantageous market position. At the same time, we recognize that our regional scope creates a continuing internal challenge to maintain a unified firmwide strategic vision that accommodates the distinctive personalities of each of our offices.

Only recently have we developed the kind of comprehensive marketing program and infrastructure necessary to address this issue on a consistent basis. Now, with the establishment of a marketing department staffed by an experienced marketing administrator in our Winston-Salem office, and marketing coordinators in Charlotte and Raleigh, we have been able to initiate a number of internal marketing activities that are increasing communication and camaraderie among all our offices.

While our internal marketing program has a number of different facets, the one that has received the most vocal approval is the development and distribution of "marketing success memos." On about a biweekly basis, one-page memos that describe a recent success story of a particular lawyer, practice group, or office are distributed firmwide. Sometimes a memo outlines a successful event that was months in the making; other times it might recount a single interesting incident.

Whatever the subject, these marketing success memos are terrific communication pieces. They spread good news that everyone might not otherwise hear. They give us an opportunity to shine the spotlight on each of our offices and on a wide variety of individuals and practice groups. They help us better know colleagues whom we might see only infrequently, and they give us a greater awareness of the diversity of matters we handle for clients. They are inspiring—and they make everyone proud to be associated with a firm at which so much great work is done.

The following is a memo that everyone enjoyed:

Although this is not Womble Carlyle's freshest (pun intended) marketing success story, the lesson it teaches is as current as the content of today's best-selling marketing manuals. I think those of you who have heard it before will enjoy the retelling. And those who haven't will be proud of the dedication it demonstrates.

From time to time, every litigator has searched through thousands of documents to find the proverbial needle in the haystack.

Several years ago, our firm persuaded an initially reluctant third party to let us examine the contents of an industrial dumpster to search for a document that could establish a solid statutory defense for one of our clients. In the height of a hot summer, this third party watched what turned into a three-day process of wading through assorted garbage in the hope of finding one magical piece of paper. His skepticism about what we were doing gradually turned into amazement and then respect for what we were trying to achieve for our client.

On the second day, he had the dumpster's contents trucked from the floor of the hot warehouse where we had been working to the air-conditioned comfort of a meeting hall in an office building. He and some of his employees even pitched in and helped, from time to time.

Eventually, our dumpster search led to a very successful result for our client. Several years later, when the third party in that matter needed corporate counsel for his growing business, he contacted that lawyer in our firm. He said he remembered being impressed by the fact that a lawyer would unflinchingly do what we did for our client. Last November, Womble Carlyle was selected over another law firm as corporate counsel for this company, and today several of our lawyers have been actively involved in matters on its behalf.

One Firm's Success Story

Lawyers:	Joseph A. Gerber and Neal D. Colton
Firm:	Cozen and O'Connor
Locations:	Charlotte, North Carolina; Columbia, South Carolina; Dallas, Texas; New York, New York; San Diego, California; Los Angeles, California; Seattle, Washington; Westmont, New Jersey; Atlanta, Georgia
Lawyers Firmwide:	230
Practice Areas:	Property Insurance Law; Subrogation and Recovery; Casualty Defense; Insurance Coverage; Arson and Fraud Defense; Environmental and Toxic Tort; Primary/Excess and Re-Insurance Claims and Defense; Professional Liability Defense; Architects' and Engineers' Errors and Omissions Defense; Agents' and Brokers' Errors and Omissions Defense; Employment Law; Directors' and Officers' Errors and Omissions Defense; Business and Commercial Litigation; Securities Litigation; RICO; Trade Secrets and Restrictive Covenants; Copyright Infringement; Construction Litigation; Lender Liability; White-Collar Criminal Defense; Environmental; Medicare Fraud and Taxation; Corporate; Real Estate; Taxation; Labor and Employee Relations; Securities; Bankruptcy; Health Care.

In 1970, the Philadelphia-based law firm of Cozen and O'Connor consisted of just four lawyers. Today, this national full-service firm consists of 230 lawyers practicing in ten offices across the United States. This story will touch on the business development and marketing components that have helped contribute to the remarkable growth and success of the firm.

Most marketing success stories have many component parts, each contributing to the positive end result. At Cozen and O'Connor, perhaps the most important component is the *attitude* of our lawyers in combination with a system that encourages and rewards the maximizing of each and every business development opportunity.

While many firms are handcuffed by origination formulas that earmark specific clients as the "property" of a specific lawyer, Cozen and O'Connor clients do not "belong" to any one lawyer. Instead, only the firm has clients. Those lawyers who work on the files, obtain the results, create the revenue, and lay the foundation for future assignments from those clients receive appropriate compensation and recognition by advancement and promotion within the firm.

This system encourages lawyers to work eagerly on each other's files, to support one another in every way possible, to team up with each other to develop new clients and new books of business from existing clients, and to search out new business development for the firm. There is never a fear or doubt that the efforts invested in business development or file handling will not be appropriately recognized and rewarded. This methodology motivates and stimulates lawyers, ensuring that everyone on board is rowing in the same direction.

At Cozen and O'Connor, business development and marketing have never been taken for granted. Each lawyer's orientation includes the following:

1. A discussion of the firm's capabilities and philosophy
2. Identification of prospective clients
3. Inquiry from the new lawyer of the identity of additional clients he or she might suggest
4. Identification of the marketing tools available within the law firm
5. Solicitation of suggestions from the lawyer as to additional or more effective marketing tools or techniques he or she might suggest
6. Identification of mentors to work with the new lawyer in demonstrating various components of the marketing plan
7. Help and support for the associate with additional training simulations, role playing, or other activities, so as to instill a sense of confidence

As each new lawyer (whether just out of law school or an experienced lateral hire) joins the firm, and as each new office is opened, serious thought is given to the business development plan. Instead of generalizations, written business development plans are created that outline, with specificity, target clients, planned activities, and calendar dates for completion.

Just as the most successful and experienced baseball team starts each season by reviewing hitting, catching, and throwing, and just as the NFL champions focus on blocking and tackling at the start of each season, so too, Cozen and O'Connor reviews the marketing game plan each year, on a practice-group-by-practice-group basis, with a focus on each component part and each lawyer's individual role.

Before opening a new office (Cozen and O'Connor has opened nine new offices in addition to its principal office in Philadelphia), considerable time and effort are invested in the marketing business plan. This written document includes all the collected intelligence on present clients located in the service area of the new office, prospective clients, books of business, and a calendar and schedule for proposed activities, including "grand opening" lunches or cocktail receptions, client calls, seminars, and other working or social gatherings. A system is then put in place to capture the information gained from each such activity and to analyze what follow-up is necessary, which approaches have proven most successful and might be expanded, and which activities are not bearing results and should either be revised or, potentially, eliminated.

Despite more than twenty-five years' success, firm lawyers continue to evaluate and reevaluate each and every component of the business development program. Accordingly, even though the firm has convened dozens of seminars in dozens of different cities, reassessment is always taking place. For example, Can we improve the seminar? Is the day of the week correct? Is the time of day right? Have we chosen the right topics and themes? Is the methodology right for the audience? Have we chosen the right venue?

Similarly, even with something so basic and seemingly mundane as announcements of new lawyers or office locations, the firm always searches out those modifications that have the potential to yield a stronger business development result. For instance, the enclosure, with the announcement, of a separate phone directory or calendar of dates or deadlines important to the clients might make a valuable addition. Another example is always assuring that, if a lawyer has significant overseas clients, a separate announcement is prepared in the native language of the clients.

In terms of an overall business development philosophy, the firm has always focused on "effective marketing." Effective marketing is defined as activities that accurately communicate information to present and prospective clients and that actually attracts clients, in the short, medium, or long term. Effective marketing has a real investment aspect to it. Care is necessary in the planning, execution, and evaluation stages to appraise critically whether the time, effort, and energy invested in each component of the marketing program is yielding appropriate returns.

In addition, while the firm moves into new geographic areas and new practice specialty areas, it shares with each lawyer a reiteration of certain basics essential to the success of a modern law firm. Here are some of those basic tenets.

We must never forget that ours is a service business. Obviously, the clients are seeking legal advice and representation. However, the end product is only one item on their wish list. Along the way, they want and deserve service and respect. Each client must be carefully evaluated in terms of specific needs and how we can best service those needs.

Moreover, while clients may or may not have the requisite sophistication to appreciate fully the quality of the legal advice rendered, most clients certainly possess more than the requisite experience to appreciate and understand whether the service measures up to the highest professional standard.

Each lawyer needs to understand that clients do not change firms only because of incorrect legal advice or a negative result. In countless discussions with the clients attracted to Cozen and O'Connor, we have learned that, more often than not, clients leave their former firm because of fundamental breakdowns in service. Failure to return phone calls promptly seems to aggravate clients more than anything else. Similarly, unanswered status requests and failure to keep the client "in the loop" also result in a move from one firm to another. Other frequently heard complaints identify a condescending attitude by the lawyers toward the clients—an attitude that is both perceived and resented by those paying the bills.

Each lawyer involved in both the marketing and the actual delivery of legal services needs to accept the reality that the attorney-client relationship is not a partnership of equals. Nothing serves the business development effort better than the enlightened view that the client is the far more important component in the attorney-client formula. Therefore, at all times, it is the client's agenda, the client's convenience, and the client's preference that are of paramount concern and interest.

Once we get beyond the basic service components of returning phone calls, responding to status requests, and otherwise keeping the client in the loop, it must be understood that doing a good job, obtaining an outstanding result, and delivering precisely what the client wants— when the client wants it—represent the best marketing tools of all.

The glitz and glamour of brochures, newsletters, white papers, and extensive advertising pale in comparison to positive results. Accordingly, those responsible for marketing need to be part of the team that monitors the actual production and delivery of professional services. At Cozen and O'Connor, each lawyer has both marketing and lawyering responsibilities. Therefore, each has a direct appreciation of the marketing function as well as a direct role in producing the kinds of professional results that rank as the best marketing tools.

At our firm, the notion of marketing is an expansive and all-inclusive one. Because each and every client contact, whether in person, by telephone, or by letter, results in the client coming away with either a positive, neutral, or negative impression of the lawyer—and therefore of the law firm—our lawyers are repeatedly sensitized to the marketing component embedded in every client contact. At Cozen and O'Connor, marketing has never been viewed as a separate or distinct activity divorced from the everyday relationships with clients. That sensitivity has inured to the firm's benefit, given the extraordinary leverage that results when each lawyer sees each client contact as having a real business development aspect. Finally, each of our lawyers is repeatedly reminded that the complaining client may be the most valuable client of all. Today the practice of law is more competitive than ever. Clients are confronted with the broadest choices imaginable. Each community seems to be populated by more and more lawyers and more and more law firms each year. Accordingly, the dissatisfied client always has the option of simply moving on to another firm. The client who takes the time and effort to voice a complaint provides the firm with extraordinarily valuable information. This client gives the firm the opportunity to remedy the problem and to demonstrate affirmatively just how committed it is to the client's satisfaction. Remember, the complaining client may merely be the tip of an iceberg, providing valuable information about potentially significant problems also affecting many other clients who have not seen fit to complain.

In conclusion, then, the secret behind the Cozen and O'Connor success story lies, in significant part, in a living and vibrant business development and marketing approach. Each and every person engaged in the business development repeatedly steps back and thinks critically and analytically about (1) what attracts clients to the law firm in the first place and (2) what keeps clients coming back. This is an ongoing process that must be applied to each component of the business development plan to ensure that the firm's vision of where it is and where it wants to go remains in clear focus.

Long-Range Planning
Is Crucial

Lawyer: Harold A. Feder

Firm: Feder Morris Tamblyn & Goldstein P.C.

Locations: Denver, Colorado

Lawyers Firmwide: 11

Practice Areas: General Trial and Appellate Practice in State and Federal Courts; Commercial and Construction Litigation; Family; Divorce; Child Custody; Personal Injury; Professional Malpractice; Products Liability; Real Property; Eminent Domain; Probate; Estate Administration and Litigation; Estate Planning; Alternative Dispute Resolution.

When you begin any marketing program, one thing you do not do is start throwing money at the wall. The first thing you do is develop a marketing plan. It helps to conduct an in-depth retreat in which you begin a step-by-step process of analyzing the strengths and weaknesses of your firm and the challenges and opportunities in your community. You proceed by categorizing what you do best, and remember the 80/20 rule—20 percent of your client base will bring to you 80 percent of your work. I began this planning process many years ago and now keep a notebook of marketing plans for the past eight to ten years. I can then refer back over the past few years and see how successful this planning effort has been. Above all else, I remember that long-range planning is critical to the marketing process. You have to decide where you want to go and how you want to grow.

Here are a few additional marketing suggestions.

1. Create a unique letterhead and always carry your logo through on everything you do.
2. Create a simple strategy to get your name out there on a regular basis. When members of our firm enter appearances in court, they not only identify themselves by their name, but they also include the name of our firm as well.
3. Become active in high-profile projects or programs. We encourage our lawyers to attend charity functions, and we routinely sponsor National Public Radio and Discovery programs. This helps to keep our name out there.

Publisher's Note: The late Hal Feder, a practicing trial lawyer for thirty-five years, lectured and wrote extensively on law practice management, trial technique, and expert witnessing.

Building a New Image

Lawyer: Pamela S. Belleman

Firm: Mays & Valentine

Locations: Richmond, Virginia; Alexandria, Virginia; Norfolk, Virginia; Virginia Beach, Virginia

Lawyers
Firmwide: Over 100

Practice
Areas: General Practice; Litigation; Corporate; Banking; Antitrust; Insurance; Bond; Securities; Trust; Estate; Tax; Labor; Bankruptcy; Real Estate Law.

A few years ago the twenty-five women lawyers in our firm decided to unite together. We had a meeting in the evening at the home of one of the women partners, and a speaker talked about the difference in men's and women's communication and management skills. We all enjoyed the meeting so much that we decided to meet quarterly. It was during one of our meetings that we decided to sponsor a conference for the business community on legal issues for women.

In May 1994 our firm sponsored the first annual conference, titled "Legal Issues: What Women Need to Know in the '90s." In planning the conference, we identified conference objectives and our target audience, which included women business owners, corporate counsel, professionals occupying mid- and upper-level management positions in corporations, hospitals, government agencies, and other institutions, and, of course, women clients of the firm.

We compiled a mailing list and sent invitations to more than 2,000 women. We also advertised in the local weekly newspaper. Several of our women lawyers also appeared on local television and radio news programs.

The conference created significant interest in the business community, with seventy-five women attending the first year. The conference included lunch, a keynote speaker, and breakout sessions. Each participant could attend two of six breakout sessions in the afternoon, dealing with issues such as flextime, sexual harassment in the workplace, legal services, and titling property.

Since the first conference was such a success, the firm sponsored a second conference in 1995, titled "Legal Issues: Knowing the Laws, Juggling the Roles." Again, we followed the same format by providing lunch, hosting a keynote speaker, and offering six breakout sessions. That year, sessions were offered on business planning, caring for aging parents, owning and leasing property, negotiation skills, domestic relations, and juvenile laws. More than one hundred women attended the second conference.

In 1996 I served as cochair of the third annual conference, the theme of which was "Business and Legal Issues for Women: Taking Risks and Reaping Rewards." At lunch there was a panel discussion featuring three prominent women business owners from our community.

Our firm has secured several new clients from these conferences, but more importantly, we have increased our name recognition in the business community and are now regarded as a leader in dealing with women's legal issues. The conference has dramatically changed the image of our firm. Before, people perceived us as not unlike most law firms, an old-line, conservative men's firm. Now, we have a much more progressive image, which benefits the firm as a whole, not just the women in the firm.

The success of the conferences has generated a number of other business development activities. In July 1994 the firm introduced "Breakfast Briefs," a quarterly networking breakfast for women featuring a woman business leader in the community as speaker. This program has become so popular that we now have a waiting list to attend. Mays & Valentine joined the National Association of Women Business Owners (NAWBO) as a corporate partner. Our lawyers serve as guest columnists for the NAWBO newsletter. In addition, in 1995 the firm sponsored "Women in the Running," a training program for women preparing to run for political office.

The management of our firm, as well as our male lawyers, wholeheartedly support our efforts. They understand the benefits that will accrue to our firm by targeting this segment of the population for special attention.

Overall, the benefits of all of these activities are that we have increased our client base, we have cemented relationships with existing clients, and we have received a substantial amount of exposure and goodwill for our efforts. In May 1995 the conference was recognized by the Public Relations Society of America Richmond Chapter with a first place award in the special events category for business and industry. I believe the biggest "marketing success" is that we have improved our overall firm image as a result of these combined activities.

The Road to Success

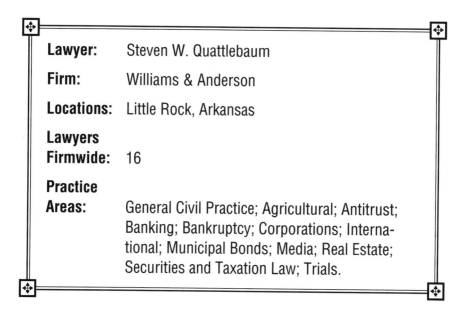

Lawyer: Steven W. Quattlebaum

Firm: Williams & Anderson

Locations: Little Rock, Arkansas

Lawyers Firmwide: 16

Practice Areas: General Civil Practice; Agricultural; Antitrust; Banking; Bankruptcy; Corporations; International; Municipal Bonds; Media; Real Estate; Securities and Taxation Law; Trials.

H ard work is the root of good representation, and it is good representation that develops business. In today's law practice, however, competition for business is intense and some marketing of one's services will aid the development of new business.

Abraham Lincoln was well respected as a trial lawyer. He frequently represented banks, railroads, and corporations as well as individuals. His advice to young lawyers about developing business is equally as appropriate today as it was in his time.

I am not an accomplished lawyer. I find quite as much material for a lecture in those points wherein I have failed, as in those wherein I have been moderately successful. The leading rule for the lawyer, as for the

man of every other calling, is diligence. Leave nothing for tomorrow which can be done today. Never let
your correspondence fall behind. Whatever piece of
business you have in mind, before stopping, do all
the labor pertaining to it which can then be done.
When you bring a common-law suit, if you have the
facts for doing so, write the declaration at once. . . .
Extemporaneous speaking should be practiced and
cultivated. It is the lawyer's avenue to the public.
However able and faithful he may be in other
respects, people are slow to bring him business if he
cannot make a speech. And yet there is not a more
fatal error to young lawyers than relying too much on
speech-making. If any one, upon his rare powers of
speaking, shall claim an exemption from the drudg-
ery of the law, his case is a failure in advance.

With some adaptation, Lincoln's sage advice is applica-
ble to the current marketplace. First and foremost, you
must provide excellent service to your existing clients. This
means much more than merely obtaining a favorable outcome in litigation (although a favorable outcome is highly
desirable). The client must know that you are responsive to
his or her needs. This ranges from promptly returned phone
calls, to reports submitted in the proper format, to acceptable billing entries. To satisfy your clients' needs fully, you
must understand the job position of, and demands on, the
person with whom you correspond.

Does the corporate representative to whom you are
responsible report to the board of directors, a manager, a
committee, the general counsel, or the president of the corporation? Does he or she report in writing, orally, or both?
How much of the report involves a legal analysis and how
much a factual analysis? Are corporate policies at issue or is
this a routine matter that will not involve a change in the

way the company does business? Too often trial lawyers do good work preparing and trying a case but fail to provide information to the client's representative that is easily usable by that person. The answers to the above questions must be known to understand fully the needs of the person to whom you are responsible.

Budget requirements are also important. Is this a routine matter that should not exceed a certain amount in litigation costs? Is it a "bet the company" case in which expense is not the issue? Does this client require an alternative billing arrangement, such as a flat fee or an outcome-related fee?

In addition, proper representation requires an understanding of the industry involved in your case. In some cases, an understanding of production methods and processes is required. In other cases, accounting procedures, wholesaling, retailing, or customer safety must be understood. Whatever the case, it is probably not the first or the last of its kind in the industry. To provide exemplary service to your client, the background that led to the particular facts should be completely understood.

The provision of such exemplary service to a client and a favorable resolution of the dispute creates a posture from which a practice may be expanded to include clients similarly situated within the same industry. A trial lawyer well-versed in the industry, with experience in an area that involves litigation arising periodically, is a commodity that is valuable and rare to the industry.

Once expertise has been acquired and excellent service has been provided, all that is required to facilitate the development of new clients is appropriate exposure. As Lincoln observed, the most effective exposure is obtained by speaking on the subject. The opportunities for speaking are readily accessible. First, check with the existing client about industry programs, meetings, and seminars. Second, identify the program directors for such events. Third, prepare materials that members of the industry will find useful and interesting. Fourth, contact the program directors, provide the materials, and arrange to speak at an upcoming meeting. Lastly, when the speaking opportunity arises, make a good presentation and provide good materials. If appropriate, follow up with the industry members who attended the meeting with an offer to present the program internally to their companies, such as to their retail managers or human resources officers.

Speaking may not be enough to develop new clients. Publish an article in the industry trade journal or magazine or prepare a monograph on the topic and distribute it to the industry. If possible, speak at legal seminars on the subject matter. Recognition in one's own field as being knowledgeable about a particular area is always positive, and word is likely to spread to the industry. Finally, do not overlook computer e-mail or databases. It may be possible to publish a short article through the computer medium.

Expanding a client base is difficult and requires work. For every ten potential clients to whom you are exposed through at least two mediums, you may get one test case to see if you can provide high-quality legal services. Diligence is the leading rule for developing a practice. No effort on your part to expand your practice will be successful if the service you provide is less than excellent. The development of a law practice begins and ends with exemplary service, and, above all else, that is the catalyst for growth. This was summed up in the words of another great president:

Never fear the want of business. A man who qualifies himself well for his calling, never fails of employment in it.

Thomas Jefferson
Letter to Peter Carr, June 22, 1792

Make Rainmaking a Priority

Lawyer: Ellisa Opstbaum Habbart

Firm: Prickett, Jones, Elliott, Kristol & Schnee

Locations: Wilmington, Delaware; Dover, Delaware; Kennett Square, Pennsylvania

Lawyers Firmwide: Over 50

Practice Areas: Delaware Corporate Litigation and Transactions; General Litigation, including Personal Injury, Workers' Compensation, Criminal, and Domestic Relations; Trust, Estate, and Tax Law; Admiralty; Business; Banking; Hospital Law; Patent and Copyright; Commercial and Residential Real Estate; Legislative Representation before the Delaware General Assembly and State, County, and Municipal Authorities.

I believe that rainmaking is crucial to a lawyer's career. To be able to "make rain" effectively, any lawyer must first be certain to provide clients with excellent service, in terms of both quality and efficiency, and be able to entertain prospective clients and attract their interest.

In addition, lawyers must never underestimate the power of referrals. There is no better rainmaking potential than when a prospective client has been told by an existing client that you did a terrific job on his or her behalf. Although I believe you must work diligently to be an expert in a specialty, that is not enough. To the extent that your clients do not or cannot let others know of your talents, it is your responsibility to do so.

Lawyers must understand and accept that any rainmaking activity requires a substantial time and financial commitment. Once you target an activity that will provide you with the means to advertise your expertise, you must be ready to engage in that activity for a protracted period of time. One or two visits to a group's meetings, participation in a single panel presentation, or one or two brief articles or rounds of correspondence is not enough to attract the attention of your audience. It is only after these efforts are consistently made over a substantial span of time that you gain credibility and name recognition. You must be willing to make personal sacrifices. Meetings and presentations may take you away from home on weekends and may require you to devote what would otherwise be personal time to your rainmaking efforts. You must throw yourself into your chosen activity and be willing to walk into a room full of strangers. Your goal must be to make those strangers into people you know. To attend and stay with people you know or with a spouse defeats the purpose. Go alone. Then you are forced to introduce yourself or spend the time standing alone and talking to yourself.

You cannot expect to see results overnight. Instead, you must think of your efforts as planting seeds in the minds of your target audience, seeds that will eventually grow. The ability to focus on long-term results is a quality that is necessary to be a successful rainmaker.

Of course, the support of your firm is crucial. The time commitment will take you out of the office. You may not be able to devote yourself to billable matters when you are involved in your rainmaking activities. This costs your firm real dollars. In addition, the cost of your rainmaking activities may be a substantial expense to your firm. Depending on how your compensation is determined, it may also affect your earnings. It is a question of what comes first, the chicken or the egg. To say that your rainmaking activities will take you away from billable work assumes that there is billable work to be done. To have the billable work, you must engage in rainmaking activities. You need to make a real commitment. If you are not as lucky as I am, you must educate your firm on the importance of such a commitment.

I believe that women can be as successful as men in rainmaking. Again, I stress that whether you can compete with the men in your firm is largely a question of whether your firm supports rainmaking activities as opposed to whether or not it supports male versus female rainmaking. If you do not care to go to the golf course, you must find alternatives and take the initiative. To the extent that many groups were traditionally made up of male members, I have found that most are making efforts to see that more women are part of their ranks. Take, for example, the American Bar Association, as evidenced by the Law Practice Management Section Women Rainmakers, the Commission on Women in the Profession, and marketing efforts to attract more women on the part of all the ABA sections. Volunteer! Make it known to those in charge that you are willing to be a hardworking and diligent member. In fact, being a woman may provide opportunities that are not available, or are less available, to your male colleagues. In addition, there are more and more women in a position to decide who is engaged to work on different matters. Assuming that your substantive skills are in place, network with these women professionals. My bet is that the working relationships you can develop with these women may be very different from those that can be developed with your male colleagues.

Of course, after the time and money have been expended, it is necessary to evaluate whether the commitment is justified. Has new business come into the firm that may be tied to your efforts? Do not evaluate just in terms of whether it has personally brought you business. To the extent that you brought in a matter within the expertise of someone else in your firm and that person was engaged, you should consider your efforts successful. Has the firm received good publicity as a result of your efforts? Have your efforts resulted in further invitations to get involved in more visible and potentially lucrative positions? Are you giving 100 percent to the effort?

In sum, serve your clients well. Even if all of those around you do not seem to make rainmaking a priority, make it yours. It is important to your professional success. Choose a target, enlist your firm's support, and make the commitment to provide as high a quality of service as you would on any billable matter. Volunteer your services and consistently participate in all of the group's activities. I do not believe that any group will turn down quality services on the basis that you are a woman. In the final analysis, it is up to each of us individually to make our own rainmaking opportunities.

Developing a
Marketing Culture

Lawyer:	Robert J. Smith
Firm:	Morgan, Lewis & Bockius LLP
Locations:	Washington, D.C.; Philadelphia, Pennsylvania; New York, New York; Los Angeles, California; Miami, Florida; Harrisburg, Pennsylvania; Pittsburgh, Pennsylvania; Princeton, New Jersey; London, England; Brussels, Belgium; Frankfurt, Germany; Tokyo, Japan; Singapore; Jakarta, Indonesia
Lawyers Firmwide:	850
Practice Areas:	Integrated Legal Services, including Business and Corporate Finance, Intellectual Property, International, Regulatory, Tax.

I would like to share some ideas about our firm's approach to marketing. Developing strong relationships with clients is the number one priority of each lawyer at Morgan, Lewis & Bockius LLP. Our watchword is "responsiveness." We return phone calls promptly, and if we can't help our clients in specific areas of expertise, we introduce them to the best lawyer who can. That is the foundation of our marketing philosophy.

The members of our firm call upon a number of institutional tools and techniques to market our firm, including those listed here.

Personal letters and newsletters.   We make certain that our clients know that we are on top of fast-breaking developments that may affect them. Many of our lawyers write personal letters to clients to keep them informed. These are personal "Dear Bob," "Dear Jane," "Dear Tom" letters that communicate developments of interest to that particular client. They are designed to supplement periodic newsletters and firm white papers that focus on particular substantive areas. In our surveys, we have found that clients enjoy reading these documents and appreciate the timeliness of the information.

Seminars.   Our firm routinely conducts seminars for groups of clients either on a firmwide or office basis. We have regularly scheduled seminars in selected areas and breakfast seminars or brown-bag lunches on critical "hot" subject areas that require immediate attention. In the latter instance, the seminars are usually small in size and selective in terms of invitees. The clients who attend exchange information and learn from one another as well as from the lawyers who are present. Inviting small groups of clients into our offices to discuss issues of importance to them has proven to be a very positive experience both for us and for them.

White papers.   Lawyers develop white papers to send to clients on substantive areas of our practice. Our goal is to let clients know that we have significant breadth and depth in our various practice groups. We are promoting the concept of an integrated firm with a coordinated approach to problem solving. No matter where a client enters our firm— whether it is the smallest or largest office or whether it is in the United States or abroad—that client will have the full range of our expertise brought to bear to solve his or her problems.

We recently did a survey of our clients to test client reaction to our white papers, newsletters, and other communication vehicles. From our clients' perspective, we discovered our communication program was effective. Clients want more information from us, not less. We asked our clients directly to evaluate our efforts in the white paper area because we believed, at the time, that the white paper system might have been too slow and ponderous. We were considering, as a result, replacing or supplementing it with more "quick hit" items. What we learned surprised us. Our clients really like our white papers. They keep them and catalogue them. They want more of them, and they want them to cover a wider variety of areas in the law. We also discovered that some wanted to receive material from us in electronic format, so we have added those clients to our e-mail system.

Firm identity. One of our most difficult marketing challenges as a firm was to crystallize who we are as a law firm. I have been serving as chair of our Firm Practice Development Committee for several years, and the "identity project" has been an interesting effort for all of us. Morgan Lewis has, like many other law firms, exploded in size. I joined our firm in 1972, and we were then the fourth largest law firm in the country, with more than 250 lawyers. At present, we have 775 lawyers, and we are still the fourth largest firm in the country. That level of growth reflects, in some respects, how the legal marketplace has changed over the past two decades.

When I joined the firm, we had traditional, clear values and benchmarks for our practice. We had standards for client service and quality work products, how we treated each other, and how we responded to client needs. As a result of our growth over the past two decades, fueled by lateral acquisitions who brought their own views and concepts of practice to the firm, we were concerned that we might have

lost our traditions and values. Through the strategic planning process of the firm and our concentration on consensus
building, however, we have spent a considerable amount of
time charting a course for the future while retaining and
emphasizing our "core" values.

Guidebook. As a corollary to the strategic planning process, our committee began working on a guide (or brochure)
designed to describe our firm. When we started this project,
we realized that the document itself had to communicate
our values and what separated our firm from others in the
legal marketplace. The process forced us to focus on,
express clearly, and write down who we were, what we
stood for, and what we hoped to be in terms of a law firm
and in our relationships with our clients.

In developing the guide, we recognized that we needed
to communicate to both the external and internal marketplace. The process resulted in the development of "A
Guide to Integrated Legal Service," which has proven to be a
very useful and popular piece. In my opinion, the document
knits everything together. It is written from a client's perspective. It provides a brief history of the firm and gives the
reader a sense of both our various practice areas and what
Morgan Lewis stands for—our core values. It includes a lawyers' directory with telephone numbers and even provides
a photo, a map, and a brief history of each of our offices.

The production process was difficult, but now we can't
keep the guide in stock or in our reception areas. It has
been widely accepted by our lawyers, who use it on a regular basis. We originally distributed it at a partners' meeting.
We then met with associates and staff in each firm office,
gave them a copy, and asked them to read and digest it.

The guide is multipurpose. It can be used for client presentations in addition to thirty to forty practice pamphlets
and lawyer résumés in a compatible folder; it can be used

for law school recruiting; and it can be used as an orientation piece for those interested in the firm—consultants or the press. The message of the guide is simple: Morgan Lewis is an integrated enterprise—whether clients are dealing with our London, New York, or Singapore office, they can expect the same quality of service and full range of resources. We can bring parts of the puzzle together and can address the client's problem, however complex, in a comprehensive and multifaceted way. The guide truly has proven to be a "realization piece."

Advertising. Now that we are communicating our image, we have felt a growing need to raise our profile in certain substantive and geographic areas where we practice. We are beginning a prototype advertising campaign because we believe that we are not as well known, as a firm, as we should be. Our goal is to raise the profile of the firm in general and the profile of individual offices and practice groups in particular. We believe that we have a unique identity, and we want to tell our story. This is a new marketing tool that we are just beginning to utilize.

Strategic alliances. In most instances, these are accomplished on a person-to-person level, but I see more and more of these being formed between our firm and other organizations. For example, we might cosponsor a seminar with an accounting or consulting firm or jointly make a presentation to a common prospect and package our collective services. We have built a variety of strategic alliances and find that this is an effective technique for both marketing and client generation. We have also developed successful referral relationships.

Client profiles. It is important in today's legal environment to know who your clients are. With multiple offices located both domestically and internationally, the challenge of cross-selling is enormous. Law firm success or failure is dependent on what you know or don't know about your client base. At Morgan Lewis, we are developing information about our clients, their structures, their locations, and the services we provide to them as well as the services we are not providing. Of course, acquiring some of this data has been difficult. Nevertheless, it provides the foundation for practice generation and cross-selling. It is often said that clients hire lawyers, not law firms. Nevertheless, if you don't know where the opportunities are—even within your own client base—you can't even enter the "retention race." As a result, we are trying to discover as much information about our client base as possible to tap effectively into our potential to broaden our existing service base.

Speech and article list. We publish a quarterly list of every speech and article written by our lawyers. This list is mailed to clients on our mailing list who, in turn, can use the list to request articles on a wide variety of topics. We receive a tremendous number of requests for these items from clients. Each lawyer who writes an article or provides a speech noted on the list receives a report showing who has requested the items. That lawyer, in turn, follows up with the lawyer responsible for the client, who also receives notification of the request to determine whether a prospect for practice expansion exists. It provides a nice blueprint for cross-selling. Again, it comes down to knowing your client and taking the initiative.

Our marketing culture. I believe that our firm at present has effectively created a marketing culture among our lawyers. We have developed a platform of tools, including a guidebook, newsletters, white papers, and speech and article lists, and we are in the process of developing a comprehensive knowledge base on our clients. In terms of marketing and practice development, we call for accountability from our partners. As such, marketing isn't just another exercise. It has become part of our culture.

A Formula for Expansion into New Markets

Lawyer: Louis B. Goldman

Firm: Altheimer & Gray

Locations: Chicago, Illinois; Warsaw, Poland; Prague, Czech Republic; Kiev, Ukraine; Bratislava, Slovakia; Istanbul, Turkey; Beijing, China

Lawyers Firmwide: Over 200

Practice Areas: Full-Service Law Firm

F ive years ago I convinced our firm to open a foreign office. Because of effective marketing, today our firm has six foreign offices and we employ one hundred people outside of the United States. We began with our initial office in Poland. We had contacts there, knew the people, and understood the region, so it was easy to achieve early success. I attribute our success with entering new markets to finding the right balance of people who make up an office. We pair the best, most-experienced lawyers who are established in the local region with a few junior lawyers who speak English, then add at least one lawyer from the United States who has a sophisticated business practice. We then send them out to market frontline work for major U.S. companies doing business internationally. We found that there is a "formula" for opening any new office. It includes the following:

1. Make it known that you are there. Use announcements, tombstone ads, press releases, etc. Most firms will make the error of announcing or publicizing a new office in their own backyard. You need to publicize your presence in the new location.

2. Don't underestimate the importance of referral and walk-in business. Ninety-five percent of our foreign clients are new clients. We don't open new offices because our clients have work in foreign countries. We open offices based on potential for developing business. We look for opportunities with Fortune 500 or major European public companies. In Warsaw, after one year we had one hundred new clients including major U.S. companies.

3. Have a good system to get the new office running. Be aware of due diligence and communication issues. Make sure you always include the name of the firm on all documents. We put Altheimer & Gray on an important international purchase agreement being prepared for a key government ministry. These forms have gone all over the world with our name on them. We get engagements left and right from this name recognition.

4. Be prepared to do some pro bono work to get established. In the Czech Republic, we sent a "rising star" partner over to work with the Ministry of Privatization on mergers and acquisition work. He was totally dedicated to them and turned down other

engagements. Because of our allegiance, we now have a thriving practice in that location.

For each of our six foreign offices, this marketing formula was successful. I spend part of my time these days looking for new markets in which to apply this proven formula.

Variety Is the Spice of Life

Lawyer: James L. Forman

Firm: Rider, Bennett, Egan, & Arundel, P.L.L.P.

Locations: Minneapolis, Minnesota

Lawyers Firmwide: Over 80

Practice Areas: Business; Litigation; Estate Planning; Trials and Appeals; Commercial and Corporate Law; Securities and Corporate Finance; Taxation; Commercial Real Estate; Health Care; Employee Benefits; Creditors' Rights and Bankruptcy; Probate; Trust Law; Labor Law; Automobile Insurance Litigation; Casualty Insurance; Products Liability; Subrogation; Fire; Construction Litigation; Liquor Liability; Transportation; Aviation Litigation; Antitrust Litigation; Securities Litigation; Environmental and Toxic Tort Litigation; Trademark and Copyright; Legislative Affairs; Workers' Compensation and Employment Law.

I believe that my marketing success has come from a variety of activities, which I can categorize into four general areas.

1. I have tried to develop a niche within our firm. I believe I am the only trial lawyer in the firm who does solely commercial litigation work. Furthermore, I have effectively positioned myself as the "emergency room" lawyer in our firm. I did one restraining order early on and now it has become a significant portion of my practice. As a result, I have started an Emergency Relief Practice Group (primarily temporary restraining orders and temporary injunctions) made up of four partners, five associates, and one paralegal. By having this group, I believe we provide very cost-effective, efficient legal representation in the emergency relief area.

2. The firm brochure has brought me business. By way of example, one of my lawyer clients in Nebraska found out about me through the firm brochure years ago. He still refers work to me on a regular basis; however, not only does he refer work to me, he has also recommended others to me.

3. I have been very active in the legal marketplace and have come to develop credibility with the practicing bar. I am the chair of the Minnesota State Bar Association Media Committee. I have been very active with the American Bar Association Young Lawyers Division as well as the Minnesota Young Lawyers. I am presently a trustee of the William Mitchell College of Law. Because of these experiences, as well as the credibility developed in my practice, I get hired to handle a variety of different cases. Most recently, I have received requests to serve as a mediator in a variety of matters, including employment, lease, and contract disputes.

4. I have received work as a result of my public service and pro bono efforts. For example, in the past couple of years, I have served as the American Bar Associa-

tion Young Lawyers Division Special Project Coordinator for a project to address the unmet legal needs of children. This project includes establishing waiting rooms for children in courthouses, sponsoring a poster campaign regarding the risks associated with handguns used around children, promoting a public service announcement about hate crimes, and creating alternative dispute programs for children in schools through peer mediation and teen courts. This work has opened up new doors and has enabled me to meet potential clients. Recently, I had the opportunity to talk with a potential client about the children's project and soon thereafter I received a new employment noncompete matter from that individual.

The Cable Television Connection

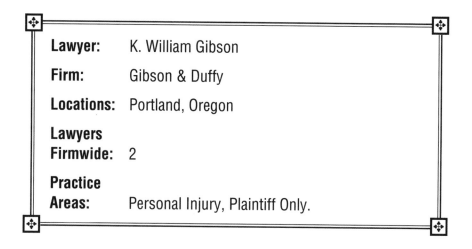

Lawyer: K. William Gibson

Firm: Gibson & Duffy

Locations: Portland, Oregon

Lawyers Firmwide: 2

Practice Areas: Personal Injury, Plaintiff Only.

O ur two-lawyer personal injury firm made its first foray into television advertising in 1990. Our commercial featured my law partner, who enjoyed local celebrity status from his four years as press aide for Portland's mayor and other television appearances.

However, after we shot the commercial, we were unsure how and where to advertise. The network affiliates had the lion's share of the viewers, but the cost of a thirty-second spot was beyond our budget. A friend suggested that we consider cable, which was a lot less expensive, so we got in touch with the company that sold ads locally for CNN, TBS, ESPN, and all the rest of the cable stations. We were concerned that cable might not have a large enough audience, but we liked the price and soon went on the air. The results were modest but encouraging.

After we had been running our commercials for a while, our account representative called and suggested that we move all of our commercials to CNN, in case something big started happening in the Middle East. (Then-President Bush had been talking for some time about the problems with Saddam Hussein and Iraq, but nothing yet had happened militarily.) Not only did we switch to CNN, but we boosted our budget at the same time. As the old saying goes, "timing is everything," and our timing could not have been better.

Within two weeks, Bush announced Operation Desert Storm and the rest is history. Everyone watched CNN for the latest news on the Gulf War and it seemed like our commercial was on all the time. (The ad rates for CNN went through the roof, but we were locked in at the old rate.) Our phones lit up with new client calls. Friends and family who had never seen our commercial called to say that they saw us on TV. Other lawyers called to comment on our new notoriety.

We let everyone think that we had figured things out on our own, but the truth is that we owed a debt of gratitude to the account representative who knew our market better than we did and had the foresight to steer us in the right direction. The message that we took away from that experience is to team up with good marketing advisors and heed their advice. Lawyers sometimes overestimate the scope of their expertise. We made that mistake, but we were given a chance to correct it.

PART 3

Niche Marketing: Positioning for Success

Five Steps to Building a Successful Niche Practice

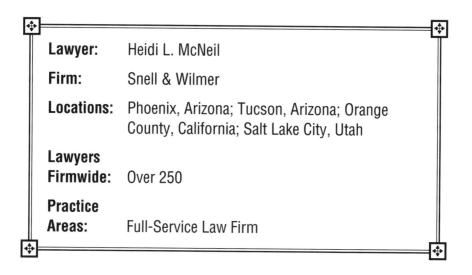

Lawyer: Heidi L. McNeil

Firm: Snell & Wilmer

Locations: Phoenix, Arizona; Tucson, Arizona; Orange County, California; Salt Lake City, Utah

Lawyers Firmwide: Over 250

Practice Areas: Full-Service Law Firm

When I began my career several years ago, technically I was a commercial litigation lawyer. Located in Phoenix, Arizona, I had an opportunity to work in the area of American Indian law. Then, a big boom occurred in the Native American gaming industry. More and more businesses were becoming involved in this area. Eventually, I created quite a niche market and developed an Indian Law Practice Group within our firm.

Here is a summary of five steps that I believe make it possible for a lawyer to build a niche practice.

1. **Get your name out there.** Participate in seminars in your desired area of practice. Write articles—let

people know who you are and what your specialty is. Think about not only the local level but about getting your name out across the country as well. Join associations in your field of expertise. Become active in the ABA.

2. **Market yourself to other lawyers—especially in your own firm.** If you effectively cross-sell yourself to other lawyers, they will effectively sell you to their clients. Make sure other lawyers in the community know what you do.

3. **Take care of the clients you do have first.** Make sure your existing clients are happy. I receive a significant amount of my new business from existing clients who make referrals on my behalf. Be accessible and be timely in responding to the needs of your clients. Return phone calls within two hours. If you cannot return the call within two hours, have your secretary place the call. Make it known that you care about the client.

4. **Deliver quality legal work.** If you don't deliver good work, you won't receive referrals. Follow up with your client once the work is finalized. Solicit feedback. Don't take your clients for granted. They can just as easily take their work across the street. Communication goes a long way. Keep the lines of communication open. Ask clients if they want to sit down and talk about how you are doing.

5. **Be cost-effective.** Don't present surprises with the bill. Make sure that you are not "over servicing." Ask clients how often they want to talk to you. Provide the level of service that they expect and can afford.

The Clients Are Contacting Us!

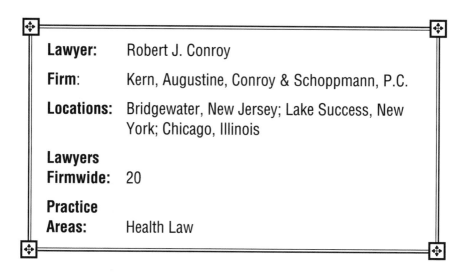

Lawyer:	Robert J. Conroy
Firm:	Kern, Augustine, Conroy & Schoppmann, P.C.
Locations:	Bridgewater, New Jersey; Lake Success, New York; Chicago, Illinois
Lawyers Firmwide:	20
Practice Areas:	Health Law

Our practice is devoted 100 percent to health care work—but more specifically, we have created a true niche in working for physicians on health care matters. Our firm is dedicated to physician work, and now we sponsor fifty to one hundred and thirty seminars per year as well as use an aggressive print media campaign strategically placed in publications catering to physicians. Our firm is also active in trade shows for the physician market.

In selecting an ad agency to support these efforts, we strategically hired an agency specializing in the physician market, not the legal market. Now the firm is fortunate to have many clients *contact us* and ask for representation.

Our innovative marketing campaign that the firm has been successfully running revolves around developing pre-paid legal service plans for medical societies in two states. As far as I know, we are the sole entity drafting and administering these plans. Thousands of members now participate and pay a yearly fee for service. It is like insurance for legal representation—all are a part of our success.

Picking a Niche

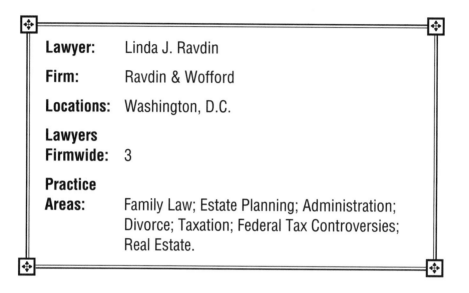

Lawyer: Linda J. Ravdin

Firm: Ravdin & Wofford

Locations: Washington, D.C.

Lawyers
Firmwide: 3

Practice
Areas: Family Law; Estate Planning; Administration;
            Divorce; Taxation; Federal Tax Controversies;
            Real Estate.

Probably the biggest concern lawyers have in starting a practice is how to get clients. Developing
business is the subject of entire articles and books. The
ABA Law Practice Management Section has published several. I will just mention a few tips that have worked for me.

First, develop a marketing plan. It does not necessarily
have to be a written plan, but at least have an idea in your
head about where you want to go and how you are going to
get there.

Second, limit your practice areas. It is tempting to take
every case that comes in the door, and in the beginning,
while *you* may be testing to see what kinds of matters really
interest you, that's okay. However, do not wait too long
before deciding what kind of lawyer you want to be and

what kinds of matters you can handle most effectively. Then stick to them and refer everything else out. Do not take cases you cannot handle competently just because you need the money. You will do a disservice to your clients as well as yourself, even if you do not get sued. You want your referral sources to know that when they send you a client, you will take care of that client. In the long term referring out a client you cannot competently represent will enhance your practice far more than you will benefit in the short term from taking the client.

By limiting your practice areas, you can then focus your marketing efforts to bring in the kind of business you want to handle. You can also focus your CLE and your substantive reading to acquire the kind of expertise that will enable you to handle the more sophisticated and more lucrative matters.

Third, ask for referrals and let others know what kinds of referrals you want. Again, limiting your practice areas can help. People who might be a source of business need to know what kind of business to send you. Moreover, if you are known to handle only a few types of matters, you will be more likely to get referrals from sources who otherwise might not send you business because you would be viewed as a competitor. Keep reminding everyone you know what it is you do. When you open your doors, send out announcements. Make them classy—classy does not have to mean expensive—and list your specialty areas. Do not say your practice area is general practice or litigation. They mean nothing.

Fourth, never leave home or the office without business cards. Consider using Rolodex cards in lieu of traditional business cards and list your practice areas on the reverse side of the cards. Take them to the beach, the ski slopes, and your nephew's bar mitzvah. You never know where your next client will be found. When you go to a professional function, put your business cards in your right pocket where they are handy. When you meet someone, get his or her card and ask what kind of referrals that person is seeking. Put the card in your left pocket, and as soon as you have a chance, write a note on the back reminding yourself where you met the person and what his or her practice areas are. Put each new person on your mailing list to be sent an announcement the next time you have something to announce. Once you ask for someone else's card, offer them yours and tell them what kinds of referrals you are seeking.

Fifth, give referrals to other lawyers. Giving referrals to other lawyers is an important marketing technique. Most people will try to reciprocate if they can. Favor with referrals those who refer business to you. When you refer business out, it sends several important messages. Many people think that if you refer business out you must be successful. Since people want to refer good business only to lawyers they think are already successful, you are sending a positive message that encourages referrals to you. Also, when you send out business that is not in your area of expertise to others with that specialty, you are letting those persons know you are not going to compete with them, and that is an incentive for them not to compete with you. In other words, if your area of practice is divorce, stick to it and send the immigration cases to immigration lawyers. They should send the divorce cases to you. On the other hand, if you get greedy and keep the occasional immigration case, the immigration lawyers have no incentive to send you divorce business. They might as well send it to someone who is not competing with them.

Finally, do not complain. When people ask you how your practice is going, say it is going great. Say you are busy all the time, but you are always looking for new clients. You do not have to be busy with clients to be busy. You can be busy reading articles, writing articles, going to CLE programs, attending professional functions, and so on. Do not imagine that if you say business is slow or your practice is developing very slowly, or, even worse, you are desperate for new business that anyone will send you a client. In fact, they are less likely to do so. People want to send business to successful lawyers, not lawyers on the verge of bankruptcy. Maintaining an upbeat, optimistic attitude will get you a lot more business than whining and begging.

The Kansas Lawyer

Lawyer: Brian F. Stayton

Firm: Blackwell, Sanders, Metheny, Weary & Lombardy, L.C.

Locations: Overland Park, Kansas; Kansas City, Missouri; Omaha, Nebraska

Lawyers Firmwide: Over 150

Practice Areas: Alternative Dispute Resolution; Antitrust; Franchise and Distributorship; Architectural, Engineering, and Construction; Banking; Bankruptcy and Creditors' Rights; Business and Commercial Litigation; Copyright, Trademark, and Intellectual Property; Corporate Law; Criminal Law; Education Law; Employee Benefits; Environmental Law; Estate Planning; Trusts and Probate; Health Law; Immigration Law; Insurance Defense; International Law; Labor and Employment; Medical Device Law; Mergers and Acquisitions; Municipality Law; Products Liability; Professional Liability; Public Utilities; Real Estate; Securities; Tax; Workers' Compensation.

I have made a conscious attempt over the past several years to position myself as "The Kansas Lawyer," especially to lawyers that I meet through the ABA on a national level. When they hear of someone who needs a lawyer in Kansas, I want them to think of me first.

I first picked up on this when my prior firm had a big client in St. Louis, Missouri. I worked with the client's St. Louis lawyer and got the case resolved. That lawyer later began calling me directly, then even tracked me to my new firm the next time he needed a Kansas lawyer. This turned out to be an important client and a real feather in my cap. Now I act as local Kansas counsel for this client because I was able to follow directions and get the job done at a reasonable rate.

In a large firm every lawyer has to develop some sort of specialty. As a general civil litigator, I realized that I could develop a geographic specialty, since I did not have a true practice specialty. So I worked to become an expert on Kansas law and started my geographic niche marketing within my firm.

I also made every attempt I could to make contacts with lawyers, both inside and outside the firm, and to make them aware of my specialized approach. I started receiving phone calls and referrals. For instance, when a new client headquartered in Nebraska needed a lawyer in Kansas to handle a case, the call was referred to me.

My advice to anyone who wants to create a geographic niche is to work every contact you can possibly make, learn as much as you can about the law in the geographic area, and be enthusiastic about your geographic niche. The people who generate business are the people who are the most enthusiastic about their work, their lives, and their practices, so let your contacts know you, your specialty, and your enthusiasm for your specialty.

Do What You Enjoy

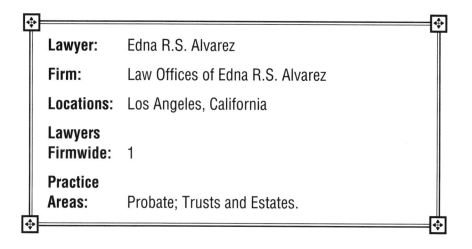

Lawyer: Edna R.S. Alvarez

Firm: Law Offices of Edna R.S. Alvarez

Locations: Los Angeles, California

Lawyers
Firmwide: 1

Practice
Areas: Probate; Trusts and Estates.

I came to Los Angeles in 1972 to practice. I did not know a single person. Twenty-plus years later, I have a very successful practice as a solo practitioner in the areas of estate planning, estate administration, and tax planning. When asked how I "marketed" my practice, I always needed to pause. In fact, I never had done marketing—as such. At least my mind-set was never that of marketing. I never participated in an activity for the purpose of generating business. I undertook an activity because I enjoyed the activity and believed in the activity—usually with great passion. I do know that whatever specific actions I took cannot be duplicated by any other person. Marketing is not a "cookbook" activity whereby one merely follows a recipe created by someone else. Marketing, if anything, is a set of activities that uniquely reflects the individual lawyer.

So the first step is to get in touch with yourself—know who you are, what your capabilities are, and what you enjoy doing. Then determine how to communicate this. My two most important sources of new clients have been existing clients and other lawyers. Because I specialize in a narrow area of the law and am a solo practitioner and thus do not have partners practicing in other areas of law, I have positioned myself as an asset to other lawyers—that is, someone to whom they can safely make a referral without concern about losing the client. I am not a competitor. I believe that both referral sources—existing clients and other lawyers—would define me as a caring person who is responsive to client needs and as an expert in a technically complex area of the law. In addition to the actual delivery of services, how did I create this "aura" of caring and competency? How did I remove the anti-solo bias (i.e., she must be a solo because she couldn't make it in the big firm arena)? How did my name become a known quantity? My "marketing" activities are in three basic areas—bar-related activities, substantive law-related activities, and solo practice-law practice management activities. As can be seen, there is overlap among these three categories.

My bar-related activities have been extraordinarily extensive and have involved service at the local, state, national, and international levels. I have served within and outside my area of specialization and at all levels from entry-level to chair. Through these efforts, other lawyers have been able to observe my high level of dedication and performance. Although a solo practitioner, my name has become well-known to many people as a result of these activities. And they are all activities about which I cared.

In the substantive law area, my activities include extensive writings on technical topics and numerous speeches in my area of expertise. In addition, I worked to become as highly credentialed as possible (e.g., the Martindale-Hubbell

AV rating, American College of Trust and Estate Counsel, International Academy of Estate and Trust Law). Finally, I served on the advisory committees of the two major estate planning annual institutes in Southern California.

In the solo practice-law practice management area, in addition to other bar activities, in the 1980s I founded the Los Angeles County Bar Association Law Practice Management Institute for Solo and Small Offices. The institute drew three to five hundred attendees per year and the promotional brochures were mailed to thousands of Los Angeles lawyers annually. I undertook this project because I felt that there was a tremendous need that was not being met. As a secondary result, the massive publicity of the institute among Los Angeles County's legal community further helped to increase my name recognition.

So, my marketing road from being a stranger in a foreign land (i.e., Los Angeles in 1972) to a widely recognized lawyer in a densely populated legal community has been to do what I enjoy, with people I enjoy, and to do it well. I have been true to myself. The client business has followed.

In the Right Place at the Right Time

Lawyer:	Michael D. Harris
Firm:	Best, Best & Krieger LLP
Locations:	Palm Springs, California; Rancho Mirage, California; Ontario, California; San Diego, California
Lawyers Firmwide:	Over 100
Practice Areas:	General Civil and Trial; Water Rights; Probate; Trusts and Estates; Labor; Corporation; Real Estate; Municipal; Public Finance; Health Care; Indian Law and Land.

It is not something I trained for in law school, but my marketing success has come from being in the right place at the right time and from developing a specialization in Native American (Indian) law.

I have an Indian law practice in Palm Springs, California, which is located geographically in the middle of the Agua Caliente Band of the Cahuilla Indians Reservation. The Agua Calientes own every other square mile of the Palm Springs area and the immediately surrounding area. Because of several land allotment programs and Bureau of Indian Affairs actions, much of the reservation has been allotted to all members of the tribe born before 1960.

In 1974 I was contacted by a tribal member and asked to represent her in dealing with a company that wanted to lease her allotted land. I told her I knew conventional real property law but very little about U.S. Trust land (reservation land). In spite of my lack of Indian law knowledge, the tribal member took a risk on my abilities. I immediately began an intense self-study and became proficient enough to warrant my client's trust. Twenty-two years later I continue to represent that same Native American woman, who has become my favorite client and good friend. In the meantime, I have become an Indian law specialist. I represent approximately fifty of the allotted members of the Agua Calientes. My practice now encompasses all areas of Indian and tribal law.

There are close to one hundred reservations in California alone. They are all sovereign nations and in many cases more efficient and economically progressive than many non-Indian political entities. I currently represent the Agua Caliente Band of the Cahuilla Indians and the Cloverdale Rancheria Pomo Makamo Indians of California. We represent the Cocapah Reservation in Arizona and have worked with the Oneida Indians of Wisconsin on special Indian Country bond financings. We have done work on many other reservations in the Southwest.

My firm also represents clients who want to purchase or lease Indian land for various projects. We represent lending institutions who want to loan money for on-reservation projects and want an opinion about whether their loan documentation is going to be valid and enforceable.

When I think about how my practice started—through a simple walk-in—I am today still grateful for that good fortune. My Native American client friend simply walked into our law office one day, and I happened to be available. She did not trust non-Indians (for good reasons); that position made my selection even more remarkable. The marketing moral of this story is that luck does play a part in our marketing efforts but the luck has to be constantly reinforced with continued attention to the law as it emerges, to producing a quality product, and to maintaining an honest and communicative relationship with the client. My client's referrals to me of other Native Americans continues to this day—sisters, brothers, children, cousins, and many other relatives and nonrelatives. Now 90 percent of my practice is Indian law–related, with 60 to 70 percent of that representing Indians versus non-Indians. I would say I was in the right place at the right time when that first client walked into our offices.

Keeping the Client Informed

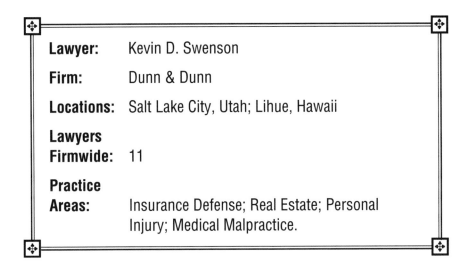

Lawyer: Kevin D. Swenson

Firm: Dunn & Dunn

Locations: Salt Lake City, Utah; Lihue, Hawaii

Lawyers
Firmwide: 11

Practice
Areas: Insurance Defense; Real Estate; Personal Injury; Medical Malpractice.

I have been practicing law for six years. The majority of my practice is in the area of insurance defense. I can attribute my marketing success to two major activities that are ongoing.

First, our firm puts out a newsletter at the end of each legislative session, which provides clients with a summary of the changes in legislation that may affect our clients in the insurance industry. This is mailed to clients as well as prospects. We always follow up the newsletter with a phone call, which is made by one of our lawyers, just to see if the recipient has any questions. This allows personal contact with a prospective client. The project is not extremely time-consuming, and it is a very effective way to keep in touch with clients and prospects.

Second, we piggyback the newsletter with a seminar, especially if the legislation is complex, or if we find that clients have questions. Generally we have about twenty-five people attend our seminars, and we have three or four lawyers speak on significant changes. All our lawyers attend to get to know clients and prospective clients and talk about the impact of the legislation in a small group setting.

We have found that by combining the newsletter with the seminar, and by directing the combination of the two at a very targeted audience, we have been able to generate additional clients. I estimate that we spend about thirty hours planning the newsletter and seminar after each legislative session. It is definitely worth the time.

Results, Results, Results!

Lawyer: Patrick J. Barrett

Firm: McGrath, North, Mullin & Kratz, P.C.

Locations: Omaha, Nebraska

Lawyers Firmwide: 75

Practice Areas: General Practice; Litigation and Appellate Practice in All State and Federal Courts; Corporate and Corporate Financing; Insurance; International Business; Securities; Antitrust; Banking; Taxation; Labor; Intellectual Property; Franchising; Real Estate; Regulatory and Administrative; Employee Benefits; Probate.

I practice in the area of labor and employment law. In our firm of approximately seventy-five lawyers, four of us practice labor and employment law exclusively. The labor lawyers participate in various seminars to provide updates to our clients, business groups, human resources associations, and lawyers. The firm's Labor Law Section drafts and mails a quarterly newsletter for our clients and others, reporting on recently enacted employment laws, court and administrative decisions, developing trends, and other matters of interest. We also publish pamphlets pertaining to a particular issue, such as the Family and Medical Leave Act and Americans with Disabilities Act. These pamphlets have been sent out to assist clients in making employment decisions affected by these laws. I understand that our clients keep them accessible and refer to them on a regular basis. Of course, this keeps our name in front of them and may generate calls to us.

Personally, the vast majority of my new client referrals comes from existing or past clients. Since our labor law practice is very specialized, especially with respect to union campaign, wage and hour, and certain types of discrimination issues, I receive many calls from other lawyers to handle certain matters for their clients in the areas in which we specialize. My marketing advice to *any* lawyer is to do a superior job for your clients to generate more clients. Firm brochures and newsletters are nice, but the best marketing tool for new clients is results, results, results!

The $64,000 Question

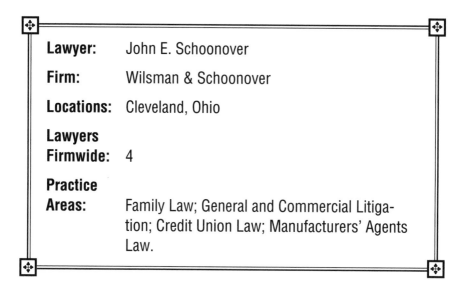

Lawyer: John E. Schoonover

Firm: Wilsman & Schoonover

Locations: Cleveland, Ohio

Lawyers Firmwide: 4

Practice Areas: Family Law; General and Commercial Litigation; Credit Union Law; Manufacturers' Agents Law.

As a lawyer, you have an opportunity to market yourself every time someone asks you, "What kind of law do you practice?" The lawyer who responds with "I have a general practice" leaves too big a net. Lawyers are much better off having a specialization and creating a twenty-second "infomercial" describing that specialization.

I began my career in a large firm and over time developed an expertise in family law and domestic relations. Once I had a clearly specialized practice, I decided it was time to open my own firm. Now 85 percent of my work is in this area. Because I am viewed as a specialist with a boutique practice, most of my work comes through referrals. Other lawyers send me work because I am not viewed as a competitor. My marketing activities are limited to participating in CLE seminars two times a year and staying in contact with my base of referral sources. By getting out in public, being friendly to people, and instilling confidence in my ability, the referrals come in. It is key, however, that people know what type of work to refer to you. You also have to remember to support the people who support you.

Creating a Boutique Law Firm

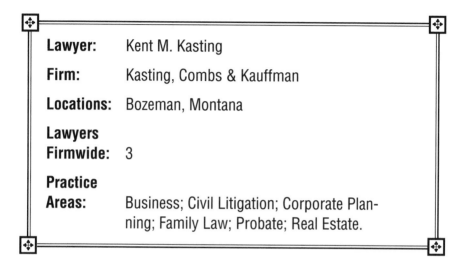

Lawyer: Kent M. Kasting

Firm: Kasting, Combs & Kauffman

Locations: Bozeman, Montana

Lawyers
Firmwide: 3

Practice
Areas: Business; Civil Litigation; Corporate Plan-
            ning; Family Law; Probate; Real Estate.

I started building my firm before I even graduated from law school. During my second year, my law school friend and classmate and I began purchasing furniture and equipment, making contacts, and generally getting the word out in anticipation of the day we would "hang out our shingles."

We signed a long-term lease for some respectable office space before we passed the bar, so once we passed, we *had* to market! We had "borrowed money" in the bank to cover those first and hopefully few lean months. We got the word out that we were ready to practice and serve clients at reasonable rates. We gradually added staff and lawyers and started building our practice.

Our marketing approaches have always been more indirect than anything. When we were young and somewhat inexperienced, we took whatever walked in the door. By building carefully and slowly, we now have the luxury of selecting the cases in which we want to be involved.

We have always tried to maintain a low overhead without sacrificing quality and technology—admittedly a difficult but nonetheless achievable goal. We wanted to achieve the goal of always appearing solid and stable but not opulent. I believe clients respect and want the former and dislike and are suspicious of the latter.

For reasons unknown to me, I gravitated toward family law, and over the years, I believe I have built a fairly good boutique practice in that area. Most lawyers do not like divorce work. I learned early on how to work effectively in this area and still avoid "Atilla the Hun" litigation techniques. I receive approximately 50 percent of my referrals from existing clients and 50 percent from other lawyers throughout Montana. My partners concentrate their practice in business, real estate, and estate planning, and consequently we together fill a unique niche in our legal community. We truly have become a boutique law firm.

Since my first year in practice, I have always been actively involved in bar work. Not only did I feel like I was doing something worthwhile, but I also met and socialized with a great number of fine lawyers, most of whom at one time or another refer their family law work to me. In addition, I have always contributed my time and talent to community, civic, and charitable organizations.

In so doing, I try to see that our firm receives ample and accurate acknowledgments for whatever community services we perform so that, it is hoped, the public can see that we do more than just practice law.

However, it is important to remember that unlimited, unmanaged public and bar service can drain your energies and become a burden if you say yes to all requests for help. Consequently, we have become more task-oriented so that we are in control of the time we give to public service. By task-oriented, I mean we become involved in specific public service projects where the amount of time to be spent can at least be estimated in advance.

We also feel that it is important to make certain that any public service is a firm, not an individual, decision. We perform a particular, focused analysis of where we want to be active so that not only will we be able to provide services that are valuable, but those services will also maximize our firm's exposure in the community.

Our practice is located in Bozeman, a small southwestern Montana town (about thirty thousand people). The practice of law is very competitive here because not only do we live and work in a very pleasant and special place, we also have an abundance of lawyers. However, the lawyers we do business with understand that we are not going to take their clients. We take care of the matters referred to us and, in most cases, the client then returns to the referring lawyer for any additional legal needs. This approach provides a mutually beneficial symbiotic professional relationship between our firm and the referring firm.

Our firm has also done some advertising in the Yellow Pages, but we ultimately concluded that this approach was not the image we wanted to convey and in fact it did not attract the type of work we wanted. Now we have only a small and dignified listing in the Yellow Pages, which conveys the message we want the public to hear—we are specialized and focused on particular areas of the law.

In terms of building a practice in a small community, we believe it is very important to develop close business relationships with as many people in the area as possible. We do our banking business with several banks. We have built strong relationships with numerous real estate agents who we trust and to whom we refer a lot of business. In turn, they likewise refer clients to us. Many of our clients are unskilled and unfamiliar with financial matters, and we like being able to refer them to bankers, realtors, CPAs, or other experts in whom we have confidence so we know they will have someone to rely on in areas where they simply do not have the requisite skills and knowledge to make good decisions.

We also believe monthly billing statements can be an important marketing tool. We are very meticulous about our billing statements and keep very detailed time records, setting out exactly what was done, said, or discussed. One of the worst things a lawyer can do is inadvertently enter a time entry that does not pertain to the client's matter or send a bill that has a time entry or cost duplicated. I personally review all statements and write a personal note on *each* statement *each* month. My notes will say things like "Thanks for the payment" or "Is there a problem with the bill?" If there is a problem over the bill in the future, I can present the client with the statements containing my repeated inquiries and invariably the client will make arrangements to see that the bill is paid. I also sign each note so that the client will know that I personally reviewed the bill before it was sent.

I believe this achieves three things. First, it creates goodwill with the client; second, it provides documentation regarding what attempts have been made to make certain that the client has no problems with the bill; and third, it personalizes the attorney-client relationship that computerized billing simply ignores. The detailed time entries also provide a source to demonstrate that things were done and issues discussed if a client ever claims you neglected to do something in connection with his or her matter.

To summarize, there are some words of wisdom that I believe make the practice of law more enjoyable, less stressful, and more professionally (and believe it or not financially) rewarding: "Good lawyers work hard, live good, die poor." I try to work hard, and I have been able to have a very nice lifestyle. I probably will pass on without having to worry about excessive estate and inheritance taxes. I enjoy what I do (at least 80 percent of the time), have never wanted for work, and have enjoyed helping people get through some very difficult times in their lives. Enjoying what you do is perhaps the best marketing tool anyone could ever present to a client.

The Field of Dreams Approach—Build It and They Will Come

Lawyer:	Kevin R. Armbruster
Firm:	Cushing, Morris, Armbruster & Jones
Locations:	Atlanta, Georgia
Lawyers Firmwide:	8
Practice Areas:	Corporations; Partnerships; Trusts; Commercial Transactions; Federal Income Taxation; Mergers, Acquisitions, and Reorganizations; Commercial Real Estate; Qualified and Nonqualified Employee Benefits and Compensation; Federal and State Securities Regulations and Estate Planning and Probate; Civil Litigation; Alternative Dispute Resolution.

T he growth of my practice has exceeded my expectations, and I attribute this mainly to hard work, client service, and opportunities in the small-firm market niche. I like my work, and I put a lot into it.

I was a CPA before going to law school. Right out of law school, I joined a large firm in its corporate and tax law department. There, I kept my hands in a lot of different areas and made every effort to work for a variety of different partners. In an evening program after work, I earned an L.L.M. in tax. I left the large-firm environment after three years with a small group of business lawyers to form a boutique firm with a general business practice (covering a broad spectrum of corporate, tax, real estate, and securities matters). We made a conscious decision at that time not to do any serious litigation, electing instead to direct our energies toward getting disputes resolved or settled as early in the process as possible and to refer intractable matters to "real" litigators, preferably in local litigation boutiques. We have continued this arrangement to the present day and have developed excellent reciprocal referral relationships with a number of litigation firms in town.

I did not join my new firm as a partner, nor did I have any business I could call my own. My incentive to leave the security of the big firm (with a first baby on the way at the time), however, was the (unwritten and unguaranteed) promise that, if I continued to work hard and develop my skills, I would be made a partner in two years (i.e., after five years of practicing law). I was told not to worry about bringing in business and that the business would come if I merely attended to these simple precepts. Two years later, I was made a partner, and ten years later, I now have a substantial and active client base made up of businesses of all kinds, including large corporations (mostly closely held, but some public), "mom-and-pop" businesses, doctors' professional corporations, and even an occasional individual with a tax or other business matter.

Each of the eight lawyers in my firm has one or more niches in the corporate market, but at the same time we all strive to be good generalists who can handle most, if not all, of our clients' needs. This, for example, enables us to respond quickly (often in the same phone call) to the client's day-to-day questions and needs, without having to bring in a specialist who is a stranger to the client (and who must be brought up to speed at the client's expense).

In my case, I began my career doing a fair amount of employee benefits and estate planning work. While this experience has been very helpful in meeting the needs of many of my closely held business clients and continues to be a substantial part of my practice, over the years the subject matter of my work has significantly expanded and diversified. My focus remains in the business area, but my practice now includes, among other areas, mergers and acquisitions, equipment leasing, software contracts, employment contracts and relations, private placements, and tax controversies. This requires a great deal of reading to keep abreast, but it makes for a very interesting and rewarding work experience. It also increases the frequency of client contact and thereby facilitates development of the client relationship.

We value our client relationships. Most of our clients know more than one lawyer in the firm. We strive to know the client and to understand and be attuned to the client's business. Many clients are considered not only clients but friends as well.

If I had to describe my firm's marketing approach, it would be marketing through good service and the client relationship. We tell our younger lawyers that they do not have to bring in business to be successful or to become a partner in the firm—they need only focus on becoming competent lawyers who can handle the client in all aspects. We believe that once a lawyer is capable of handling client files competently and independently, he or she will develop business in the natural course of things. You could call it the "Field of Dreams" approach—build the field (i.e., through hard work, competence, and dedication to service), and the clients will come. This philosophy has certainly held true in my case.

My (and my firm's) work has mushroomed in recent years. A number of factors have contributed to this. We maintain a very high standard for work product. We strive to give the clients what they want and need without "overlawyering" the matter. We provide big-firm expertise and experience with the low-overhead cost structure of a small firm. We don't have superfluous personnel, and we don't double-lawyer deals unnecessarily. And we have developed a reputation for these things in the local business community (with, among others, referral sources such as other lawyers, CPAs, and insurance professionals). Looking back, we have benefited from the domino effect—one satisfied client or professional introduced us to another, and so on.

Occasionally I provide some advice without expectation of payment. This means a lot to businesspeople used to receiving large invoices from lawyers at the drop of a hat, and they remember you for it. One contact (who later became a client) sent me a significant matter two years later because he appreciated some simple advice I had given him without sending a bill. Clients want to know that you are in it not just to bill the hours.

I have many more stories, but they all follow the same theme: Work hard, be a good lawyer, be responsive (e.g., return all phone calls before you leave the office each day or have your secretary do it), and be reasonable with your fees, and your practice will grow.

Market Your Interests

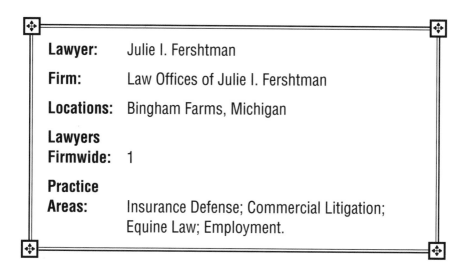

Lawyer: Julie I. Fershtman

Firm: Law Offices of Julie I. Fershtman

Locations: Bingham Farms, Michigan

Lawyers Firmwide: 1

Practice Areas: Insurance Defense; Commercial Litigation; Equine Law; Employment.

I believe that to be successful, any lawyer has to think about the law as it relates to them personally. I have always had an interest in horses and horseback riding. When I graduated from law school, I moved back to Michigan and went to work for a large business law firm. Five years ago I decided to try to merge my love of horses and law, so I did some research on equine-related issues and thought about how I could integrate this into my regular practice. Today almost 75 percent of my business is equine related. To put it simply, I took a step-by-step approach to building a new solo practice on my own largely devoted to this area, and I can share the following suggestions to anyone who wants to develop their own niche practice.

Evaluate your target market. Learn what legal issues are important to that market. Decide first who your desired clients will be. Will they be individuals (e.g., divorce and personal injury), an industry (e.g., insurance companies, banks, manufacturers), a specific segment of an industry (e.g., equine insurers, stables, etc.)? Knowing this is the first step to your marketing plan. I selected equine-related businesses and insurers and proceeded from there.

Organize your office operations. After you have evaluated your preferred areas of concentration, organize your *entire* operation to be consistent with the clients you want to serve. The type of clients you aim to serve could directly influence your choice of office equipment and services such as type of letterhead, use of voice mail as opposed to an answering machine, printers, copiers, and office location. If you want to attract business clients, particularly if you are a solo practitioner, your equipment, letterhead, phone service, and facilities should be first-rate.

With a busy practice and many commitments you will need to be very organized. I personally recommend electronic organizers like the Sharp Wizard™ or Zaurus™ or Psion™. You can take these with you wherever you go and have instant access to your Rolodex, schedule, to-do lists, and other important information.

Consider your billing rate. Carefully consider how you will price your services. Particularly if you are an experienced lawyer, setting your hourly rate too low could signal desperation or inferior quality. It might pay to send a message that you are good and worth the cost. Consider sending very detailed bills; your clients will rarely, if ever, complain.

Advertise. Do not hesitate to develop tasteful, professional advertisements. Develop an advertising budget and evaluate what publications will be worth the price. Reevaluate your advertising strategy and budget each year. I listed my services in trade-specific publications and was immediately contacted by an insurance company to represent it. After I had the first case, it gave me the ability to approach other companies in the industry.

Write. This is free advertising. If you enjoy writing and write well, develop articles for the publications that people in your target market often read. I am now publishing five years of my industry-related articles in a major book called *Equine Law and Horse Sense.*

Give speeches. This is a good long-term investment, if done right. If time allows, speak wherever and whenever you can, as long as your target market will be in the audience. When time is valuable, be selective. Give everyone a good quality handout that summarizes the speech and includes information about you and how you can be contacted.

Cultivate valuable contacts. You will develop your practice by "networking." There is no magic to the term; networking is merely placing yourself in situations where you will meet others who might be clients or refer clients to you. Your contacts might surprise you, too. (One of my contacts got me and my law practice featured on page one of the *Detroit Free Press* Business Section in December 1994; another contact got me featured on the TV-2 Detroit News in January 1995.)

Follow up with your contacts through occasional calls, lunches, holiday cards, and the like. I try to send a quarterly letter with new developments and updates to selected people on my mailing list. Always send a personally written note of thanks to anyone who refers business to you. I developed a list of twenty or so contacts and sent letters and a high-quality brochure I wrote, titled "A Horse Facility's Guide to Avoiding Liability," which has helped me secure many successful business clients.

Understand the business of your target market. Make it a regular practice to keep up on the latest information and developments. Track industry trends. Stay one step ahead of your competitors. Then read and write about the newest developments before everyone else. Regularly read trade and industry publications. Share important articles of interest to your clients. Publish articles in these publications. Let the publications know you are available to give quotes or to assist with articles on which they may be working.

Attend the major trade and industry conventions that attract people in your target market, even if this means spending a few days out of town. You will make very valuable contacts and, in time, you might be invited to speak there.

Provide top-quality service. You will keep the clients you have attracted and get referrals if you demonstrate top-quality service. Be civil and professional in your law practice. Professionalism and civility will benefit you as a person and as a lawyer. Also, you will earn the respect of opposing counsel who could, down the line, refer you business.

Sustain your efforts. Remember that sustained exposure to your target market works best. Make it a daily practice to devote time to marketing, whether through a call, lunch, letter, article, or the like. Don't stop, even if you are seeing good results. Competition is fierce. Your clients, especially businesses, may be "courted" by others.

Where possible, look for cutting-edge developments within your selected areas of practice. Be the first to develop your knowledge of these developments. In my experience, I recognized a trend in liability legislation involving equine activities and through articles and speeches have became a nationally known expert on these issues. This has boosted my practice considerably, especially the insurance defense and litigation consulting business.

These marketing tips have worked well for me. I am not only litigating cases in Michigan, but I am now being contacted by out-of-state insurance companies, businesses, and lawyers as well to provide consulting services.

Developing "Healthy" Client Relationships

Lawyer: Richard G. Cowart

Firm: Baker, Donelson, Bearman & Caldwell

Locations: Jackson, Mississippi; Memphis, Tennessee; Nashville, Tennessee; Chattanooga, Tennessee; Knoxville, Tennessee; Johnson City, Tennessee; Huntsville, Tennessee; Washington, D.C.

Lawyers Firmwide: Over 200

Practice Areas: General Practice; Civil Trial and Appellate Practice before all State and Federal Courts, Administrative Agencies, and Commercial Arbitration Forums; Antitrust and Trade Regulation; Banking and Finance; Bankruptcy; Commercial Finance; Communications; Construction; Corporations; Employment and Labor; Entertainment; Environmental; Estate Planning and Administration; Family Law; Franchising; Health Care; Intellectual Property; International Law; Litigation, including Commercial and Business; Personal Injury; Products Liability and Professional Malpractice; Mergers and Acquisitions; Municipal Finance; Municipal Law; Partnerships; Pensions and Employee Benefits; Real Estate Development; Securities; Federal, State, and Local Taxation; Tax-Exempt Organizations; Utilities; Zoning and Land Use Law.

I am a member of a very successful health law practice group that is driven by the following marketing principles.

MARKETING MUST BE DISCIPLINED AND ORGANIZED

We organize our health law group based on the clients we serve, not on the substantive expertise (e.g., tax) we may have as lawyers. We learned early on that if a client has a need we have to be part of designing the solution to solve that need, not merely the scriveners who reduce it to writing. We understand the health care industry as well as our clients do. We know the terminology; we know the key relationships. We can anticipate what our clients need early and have a team in place to serve them.

To market effectively, you begin by planting seeds. I personally have never gotten a single significant client from a dinner, lunch, or speech. You have to know what the client needs and plant a seed about how to address the need or how you have helped another client address a similar need. I am an information junkie and probably regularly read fifty health care periodicals. Of course, I give speeches, write columns, and teach at the university, but my clients hire me because I understand their business. If you are close to your clients, you know what is going on in their industry.

ACCEPT OWNERSHIP

When clients call with a problem, they are put in touch with a human being who can help them begin solving their problem immediately. We don't let clients get stuck in voice mail or on someone's trial calendar. To do this effectively, you have to have a team that can work together, with a triage system in place. If it is an emergency, the client has to be served immediately, and with a team system we can work together to identify those clients who need the most immediate attention. We all wear pagers and are accessible twenty-four hours a day, seven days a week. I would describe our environment in health care terms as a "STAT" environment. And as a team, we are not proprietary with our clients.

LEADERSHIP IS IMPORTANT

If you align yourself with only the best clients—those with the strongest reputations and resources—that gives you the edge you need. If you create a critical mass of "signature" clients, and develop career relationships with them, you will be able to develop new client relationships easily. Two-thirds of our work is institutional work and we can predict where 80 percent of our work will come from next year. We openly discuss our relationships with our clients and talk about how we can better develop and manage those relationships. Because we work with the best hospital system in one state, for example, we can learn from our experience and their experience and truly add value to our clients in other states. The best surgeons are the ones who perform a surgery over and over. Because we have bought or sold over forty hospitals in ten states, we have become more to our clients than just a cost of doing business.

One story comes to mind here. We were doing work for a pharmaceutical management company in California. Eventually this turned into work in fifteen states. I called my client in Los Angeles one day and asked him why he was using a firm in Mississippi to do his local work in Los Angeles, and he replied, "You guys respond as quickly and are 50 percent cheaper than the firms in Los Angeles and you give us advice that is as good . . . your firm is the Wal-Mart of law firms!" While I was initially offended by this reference to a discount retailer, I realized that he was complimenting us on our ability to deliver quality service at a good value.

LEARN FROM OTHER INDUSTRIES

When I look for marketing ideas, I don't look to other law firms but instead to other industries. I have primarily studied the health care industry.

Through research, I have come to realize that our firm holds the market position of the step-up law firm in the South. We have 230 lawyers spread out over eight cities, and we are positioned to serve effectively clients who are outgrowing their present firm. We have a list of potential signature clients identified in each market we serve. In the health care business, where new conflicts are emerging overnight and where business relationships are changing dramatically, many lawyers are getting displaced by the marketplace. You are bound to lose a few clients, so you had better be out there gaining a few.

Understand Your Clients

Lawyer:	M. Christine Carty
Firm:	Schnader, Harrison, Segal & Lewis
Locations:	New York, New York; Philadelphia, Pennsylvania; Washington, D.C.; Harrisburg, Pennsylvania; Norristown, Pennsylvania; Pittsburgh, Pennsylvania; Atlanta, Georgia
Lawyers Firmwide:	Over 200
Practice Areas:	International; Corporate; Labor and Employment; Litigation; Franchise and Distribution; Maritime; Real Estate; Securities; Antitrust; Tax Law.

My practice development efforts involve several developing and overlapping strands, with three main areas of emphasis. I am a commercial and employment law litigator with an interest in feminist issues and matters. My practice today consists of representing several not-for-profit women's organizations across the country, coupled with a significant amount of labor and employment litigation. For me, this brings both balance and depth to my clients.

How do I market myself? First, I actively let it be known that I like representing women and that I have a complete understanding of their issues. Although I am not really perceived as a "nurturing" type, I have a definite understanding and sense of where women's concerns lie, and I can effectively speak their language. I have the ability and perception to go beyond their concerns as women to address their business concerns. Consequently, women have become a very large target group for me, and I truly enjoy my work in this area. I continue to target women as clients because they resonate well with me. While they are not my only clients, I believe that I have become recognized for developing a practice in this area. Although a great deal of my marketing time is devoted to building relationships with clients and potential clients, I try to speak and write articles frequently on topics of interest to women. I routinely ask my existing clients and contacts to refer work to me, and these individuals know that I want to continue building a practice in this area.

To a certain extent, I target women in-house counsel, and I have had work referred to me from former in-house lawyer adversaries. I maintain two lists of client development opportunities: a comprehensive mailing list of past, present, and potential clients, and a list revised annually or every six months of one or two immediate targets.

Competition in New York City is very intense so that attraction of clients by being one of the top five or ten lawyers in a specialty is very difficult. To market effectively, I depend on personal contacts, solid legal work, and good service. I do my best to maintain cordial relationships with my clients. Unlike a handful of lawyers in New York City, I can't depend on a reputation to bring in business. What I can depend on is the fact that I bring to my assignments a practical bent—people skills, problem-solving abilities, and a personal interest in my clients and their businesses. I don't have a long learning curve when I am working with a client in the labor and employment area or in serving in a general counsel role for one of the many women's organizations that I represent. I have many clients whose general counsel are males, but since I have been very successful working in the women's area, and feel that I have a real understanding of the concerns of my clients in this area, I plan to continue my work in this area and hope to continue to expand my practice.

It's a Woman's World

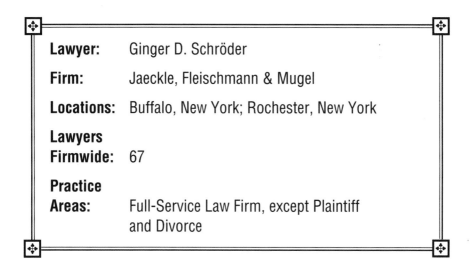

Lawyer: Ginger D. Schröder

Firm: Jaeckle, Fleischmann & Mugel

Locations: Buffalo, New York; Rochester, New York

Lawyers Firmwide: 67

Practice Areas: Full-Service Law Firm, except Plaintiff and Divorce

I have targeted 50 percent of my marketing efforts to women in decision-making positions. In my area of practice, labor and employment law, many potential clients are human resources executives, vice presidents, CEOs, CFOs, or in-house counsel—positions that are often occupied by women. My firm formed a women's marketing team and we meet on a regular basis to strategize about what groups we should join, to identify the specific prospects we should market, to brainstorm cross-selling ideas, and to talk about and work through particular problems that women lawyers may face in marketing their services or the services of their firm. This group stays on top of local events and we become involved in those that have meaning to us, clients, and potential clients.

A recent marketing success occurred with the largest privately held company in western New York. This company has thousands of employees all over the country, and we felt that they presented a wonderful business opportunity with respect to labor and employment law representation. This particular potential client had a woman general counsel. Many other law firms and male lawyers had been marketing to this company for many years. I and a woman partner in my firm had worked over a period of two years to get our names and the name of our firm in front of this general counsel. Although making the telephone call for a luncheon appointment was a little nerve-racking at first, it was easy to begin building a relationship with her. We were able to find out what her business interests were as well as her goals for her office, and we learned more about her on a social level. I now work closely with the company's in-house labor counsel—also a woman! With 30 percent of lawyers being women, it is very helpful to market yourself to others who share your same mind-set.

Networks Work

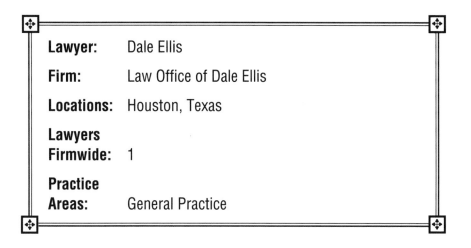

Lawyer:	Dale Ellis
Firm:	Law Office of Dale Ellis
Locations:	Houston, Texas
Lawyers Firmwide:	1
Practice Areas:	General Practice

I t was clear to me when I opened my practice that, because there are between sixteen thousand and eighteen thousand lawyers in Houston, I would have to evolve my practice so I could stand out from the competition. I decided to run an ad in the Yellow Pages, focusing on collections work. Then I joined the National Association of Collection Attorneys, a network of lawyers united to serve banks, collection agencies, credit unions, and the Visa bankruptcy protection programs. Joining the network helped a great deal through word of mouth. After joining the network, I sent letters and résumés off to companies, like Visa, requesting that when they have business in Houston, they should call me.

Now I receive referrals from around the country as a "Visa lawyer," and I am involved in six or seven collections networks, many of which serve employers such as AT&T, Aetna, and hospital groups through established prepaid legal plans. To gain additional credibility, I write and publish articles in The Practical Lawyer, for the local bar association, and for many other publications around the country. Collections work is now 25 to 35 percent of my business. Networks work!

PART 4

Client Service: Building and Maintaining a Client Base

Effective Cross-Selling
Begins with an Introduction

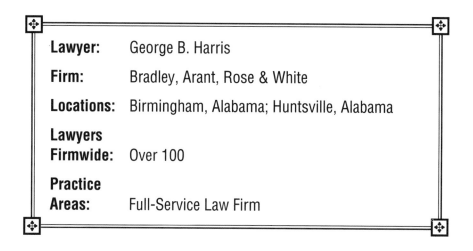

Lawyer: George B. Harris

Firm: Bradley, Arant, Rose & White

Locations: Birmingham, Alabama; Huntsville, Alabama

**Lawyers
Firmwide:**   Over 100

**Practice
Areas:**   Full-Service Law Firm

I have been able effectively to cross-sell additional services to my clients, which our firm provides. I like to have a hands-on approach to clients' legal situations and really spend a great deal of time learning about their businesses, which gives me an opportunity to expand our firm's client relationships to include other areas of practice such as estate planning, employment matters, and general corporate law work.

Closely held businesses need practical solutions to a lot of legal issues, and small business owners have a network for support. They talk to one another, particularly within their own industries, and I notice the same lawyers often representing several clients in the same industry. Look for opportunities to develop an expertise in an industry so that your clients will refer others to you. As you get to know the clients you work with day to day, look for opportunities to learn more about their business and legal needs. Do not be afraid to review with them additional services your firm has to offer as you learn of new challenges your clients face. It may be just what the client needs. Be aware of changing situations in your clients' business or personal lives. This is the time they may need additional legal services.

Always introduce someone else in your firm to your client. This is an opportunity to introduce your client to other services offered by your firm and to give the client another contact within your firm from whom to seek assistance if you are not available. If appropriate, demonstrate to your clients that your firm has expertise in other areas and is available to help them. If you are aware of your clients' business and legal needs up front, you can protect them and look out for their interests prospectively as opposed to responding to their crises. Everyone will benefit from this type of marketing approach.

Little Things Mean a Lot

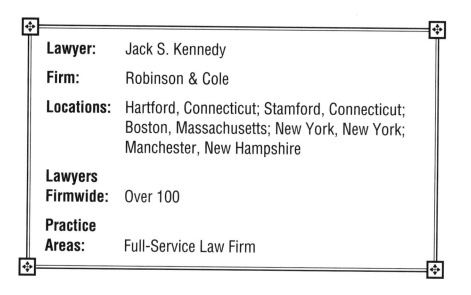

Lawyer: Jack S. Kennedy

Firm: Robinson & Cole

Locations: Hartford, Connecticut; Stamford, Connecticut; Boston, Massachusetts; New York, New York; Manchester, New Hampshire

Lawyers Firmwide: Over 100

Practice Areas: Full-Service Law Firm

O ur firm made a pricing decision to stop billing for most ancillary services—routine telephone charges, copying, faxing, postage, and the like—and it has translated into a very positive marketing technique. Our clients are very pleased. Our idea was to get rid of the small stuff. When clients are billed for a significant amount, they don't expect to see internal overhead items on their bill. Word processing charges were the most unacceptable charges in the eyes of the clients, and in the eyes of our own lawyers. Preparing documents seemed to most people a clear cost of what lawyers do.

Our policy states the following:

Ancillary Services—Nonbillable

We do not bill clients for routine telephone charges, copying, faxing, postage, word processing, secretarial overtime, or travel costs of our lawyers to other firm offices. We do bill, at our cost, for extraordinary expenditures such as conference calls and extensive long-distance and international telephone charges, large copying jobs, filing fees, messenger and courier services, and computer research charges, as well as travel and overnight expenses if specifically related to client matters. When using third-party services, we endeavor to work with the best quality, lowest-priced vendors.

I estimate that this new policy will cost us roughly $200,000 to $250,000 a year, so in the aggregate, it is not a small step. Computing our loss is not yet an exact science, but I believe clients will continue to respond favorably. Overall billing for these services was a diversion and an invitation to have clients focus on relatively minor items that don't have anything to do with the quality of our service and the positive relationship we like to maintain with our clients. So I believe that little things do mean a lot when you are saving your clients money!

Using a Bedside Manner

Lawyer: Robert D. Rachlin

Firm: Downs Rachlin & Martin

Locations: Burlington, Vermont; Brattleboro, Vermont; St. Johnsbury, Vermont; Littleton, New Hampshire

Lawyers Firmwide: Over 50

Practice Areas: General Practice; Banking and Insurance; Captive Insurance; International; Corporation; Taxation; Public Utility; Securities; Real Estate; Construction; Estates; Trusts; Probate; Legislative; Governmental Administrative; Environmental; Employment and Labor Relations; Employee Benefit; Products Liability; Professional Liability Law; Trials in All State and Federal Courts.

In my view all successful lawyer interactions boil down to communication between humans. This seems like a commonplace, but it is my experience that many lawyers view clients like the stereotypical physician to whom Mrs. Smith is "the gall bladder in 447." Marketing yourself to a client is a process of convincing the client that your perception of his or her problem is broader and wiser than his or her own. This is another way of saying that you

185

186 CLIENT SERVICE: BUILDING AND MAINTAINING A CLIENT BASE

see the client's problem not in isolation but in the context of the whole person. And the "whole person" embraces not only the client's legal travails but all other aspects of the client's life and personality.

An example that comes to mind from my own practice is a software designer who had a bitter dispute with a world-wide distributor of his product located in the United Kingdom. When he came to me, he simply wanted me to force the issue via a lawsuit. As I developed an understanding of his problem and, more importantly, got to know him, it became evident that he and his distributor had a community of interest and that the root of the dispute was more personal than business. This led me to suggest a face-to-face meeting with the "adversary," not in a law office or a hotel room but in a country inn. That venue and the opportunity for the parties to meet face to face resulted in a settlement that was a win-win situation for everyone, achieved at a fraction of the expense and torment of a lawsuit. This happy outcome led to further licensing work from the client as well as our engagement in connection with his tax and estate problems. Had we simply viewed him as "the gall bladder in 447," we would have instituted the suit (which would still be going on), and several years and a few hundred thousand dollars later, the client might or might not end up with the result he wanted. However, the alternate approach was only possible by getting to know the client beyond the confines of what he believed his problem to be and what he supposed the solution to be.

I encourage younger lawyers to make a point of getting to know their clients, not necessarily socially but in enough depth to be able to view their problems in context. If the client is a company, it is helpful to visit the company, see the workplace, get a feel for the company and its business. While it may seem peripheral to marketing, I cannot emphasize too strongly the importance of attending to the lawyer's own intellectual life through wide reading, cultural endeavors, and other means whereby the lawyer gains a superior understanding of the range of human personalities and situations. By these means we bring a broad perspective to our clients' problems and enhance our reputations as wise counselors. Such marketing is, in my view, far more effective than seminars, newsletters, brochures, or explicit advertising.

Give Something
Back to Clients

Lawyer: John L. McClaugherty

Firm: Jackson & Kelley

Locations: Charleston, West Virginia; Martinsburg, West Virginia; Morgantown, West Virginia; New Martinsville, West Virginia; Charlestown, West Virginia; Clarksburg, West Virginia; Parkersburg, West Virginia; Lexington, Kentucky; Washington, D.C.; Denver, Colorado

Lawyers Firmwide: Over 150

Practice Areas: Natural Resources (Coal, Oil and Gas, Metals, Aggregates, and Other Minerals); Admiralty; Environmental; Labor and Employment; Legislative Services; Litigation (including Administrative, Civil, Insurance Defense, and White-Collar Crime); Pension and Benefits Programs; Occupational Safety, Injury, and Disease; Workers' Compensation; Business and Commercial; Banking; Bankruptcy; Public Finance; Corporate; Health Care and Hospitals; Public Utilities and Motor Carriers; Real Estate; Securities; Taxes; Trusts and Estates; Antitrust; Administrative; Transportation; Construction; Public Agencies; Insurance Regulation and Delinquency Proceedings; Venture Capital.

I believe that any lawyer can improve marketing and client relations techniques. There are five things that I consider key to attracting clients.

1. Be a good listener. One of the biggest problems that lawyers have is that they are not good listeners. Listening is key to the formation of a relationship with your client.
2. Develop a reputation for solutions. Clients are looking for creative solutions to their problems. Don't be a lawyer who looks for reasons why a client can't do something. Instead, focus on creating opportunities and developing strategies that will enable your client to do properly the things that he or she wants to do.
3. Build relationships. Market yourself and your firm so as to build lasting relationships with clients. Learn as much as you can about the client's business. Ask your client to take you on a tour of his or her place of business. Don't insist that clients come to see you. There is simply no substitute for having an interest in your client. By taking an interest in your client, you can help the client to be more proactive, which in turn helps the client avoid legal or business problems. Ask your clients to put you on their mailing lists for press releases, announcements or newsletters. This provides a flow of information about a client's business.
4. Get out in the community. Lawyers need to be out in the community trying to make it a better place through community service.
5. Be a hard worker and deliver high-quality work.

One example from my own experience: One of our lawyers was approached by two individuals to do a private

placement of stock for a company that was to be incorporated in West Virginia but located in another state. Our firm
was about $20,000 into the matter when one of the individu-
als became very ill. We were in the middle of the transaction, but because of the illness we could not move forward.
Our firm chose to write off the $20,000 rather than to bill it to
the remaining partner. The man never forgot this, and when
he was later involved with another business, he referred
that entity to us and it became a very good client. I know
that this work would not have been referred to us had we
not treated this individual so well in years before. We effectively showed that we were interested in giving as well as
receiving.

A Successful Client Survey Program

Lawyer: O. Wayne Corley

Firm: McNair Law Firm, P.A.

Locations: Columbia, South Carolina; Charleston, South Carolina; Georgetown, South Carolina; Greenville, South Carolina; Hilton Head Island, South Carolina; Myrtle Beach, South Carolina; Spartanburg, South Carolina

**Lawyers
Firmwide:**   Over 75

**Practice
Areas:**   Administrative; Admiralty; Antitrust; Aviation; Banking; Bankruptcy; Civil and Criminal Practice in All State and Federal Courts of Record; Communications; Corporate; Environmental; ERISA; Estate Planning; Health Care; Immigration; International; Interstate Land Sales; Labor and Employment Relations; Legislative (National and State); Mergers and Acquisitions; Municipal Finance; Probate; Real Estate; Regulatory; Securities; Tax; Utilities Law.

Our firm was formed in 1971 when Robert E. McNair completed his term as governor of South Carolina. I was the legal assistant to the governor, and as he left office he invited me and Jim Konduros, his executive assistant, to join him in establishing a new law firm in our capital city. The former governor was, and is, an extraordinary business developer. I brought to the new firm organizational and management skills as well as statewide business and political contacts. Jim's strength was his strong personal relationships and credibility with governmental agencies, on the local and national level, as well as his business and political contacts. We felt we had all the components necessary for a successful law practice in the 1970s.

In the early years of the firm, our emphasis was on "doing" our clients' work, and there was very quickly more of that than the three of us could handle. With the exception of what the governor did as a natural course, there was no emphasis on client development, nor was there a need to understand what clients really were looking for in a law firm. We just did what we did well and the work kept on coming.

We were extremely successful, expanding from 3 to 115 lawyers and from one office to eight in two states and Washington, D.C. The governor as senior partner ran the firm, as one of our senior partners remarked in 1989, as a "benevolent dictator." By 1990 we knew it was time to do succession planning and the evaluation process that must precede that. We employed a consulting firm to assist us in creating our first phase of this restructuring, which was a corporate management structure consisting of a managing partner and a five-member executive committee. Additionally, we organized the firm into three broad practice areas with practice chairs appointed to manage each area firmwide. After two years and a close scrutiny of this structure, we found that it was not working for our firm. We returned to the governance/management structure of an elected managing partner with complete authority and autonomy, retaining the practice chairs but changing the scope and definition of what they managed.

As managing partner, I wanted to know what our clients really thought about the firm. I also recognized that in this day and time, in our profession, we need to understand fully what each client's unique needs are—centering on "service" to our clients, not just "doing" their work. With the help, once again, of our consultants, we planned and conducted a client survey and implemented a follow-up program.

In my view, our client survey program has proven to be extremely successful. We personally interviewed thirty of our clients, purposefully including diversity in size, geographic location, and legal services required. As managing partner, I was involved in a majority of the face-to-face interviews. Simultaneously, we mailed out questionnaires to approximately 250 of our clients representing all disciplines in our firm—litigation, finance, corporate, labor, administrative, regulatory, and so forth—which completed questionnaires our consultants reviewed and evaluated for us.

What did we learn? Several things—some good, some not so good, and some of which we were totally unaware. A respectable number of our clients could not say enough positive things about us, the quality of our work, and the responsiveness of the members of our firm. Others revealed things that I believe they never would have revealed had they not been included in the client survey process. Still others wanted changes as simple as different billing formats, or task-based billing formats, or as challenging as a fee-based incentive program. We also learned from some of our clients, without them actually telling us, that they considered their business portable and if the lawyer who was providing the primary service to the client left the firm, the client would go with that lawyer rather than remain with our firm.

Overall, I am satisfied that our client survey program has paid for itself, both financially and in building positive client relationships. Our clients told us in no uncertain terms how we could expand our working association with them and how we should focus our firm's client development efforts to accomplish that. They told us, we listened, and we are acting on what was said.

As an additional bonus during this process, we learned a lot more about us as a firm. For instance, we found that we had a group of young lawyers, and some older ones, who were not comfortable doing business development, primarily because they had no idea or training in how to develop client relationships. We instituted a business development training program consisting of fourteen sessions with behavior modeling and video instruction to train selected lawyers in successful techniques to be used in developing new and enhancing existing client relationships. We know that the old 80/20 rule applies and ultimately the relationships our firm has with its clients will determine our future success. This training program is organized and run by our business development director (a nonlawyer), who trains lawyers to lead the training sessions. The leaders generally are those lawyers within the firm who already possess good networking and business development skills and who are then trained in the process of teaching others those skills. We started this program in 1994 as a voluntary program for younger partners and associates. We are now in the process of planning additional sessions, which may be mandatory for three-to-five-year associates. It has been a very positive program with measurable results.

As a firm, we expect involvement in community, civic, charitable, professional, and trade organizations. We encourage members of our firm to write, to speak, and to provide pro bono services in each local community in which we have an office. Our director of business development assists all of our lawyers in establishing contacts as well as providing materials and information for programs or presentations.

We still, however, maintain a very conservative approach and are very selective about public relations matters. We choose to limit, and to measure very carefully, those items that we release as public promotion and in what publications we do so.

While we have not perfected our client development techniques, we have learned that each of our lawyers is unique in the way he or she attracts or maintains business. We are trying to appreciate and support those differences and encourage each lawyer to approach client development in a way that is comfortable and works for her or him.

We have to really know our clients and their needs. The bottom line is that if we don't take care of our clients, someone else will.

Love and Live with
Your Clients

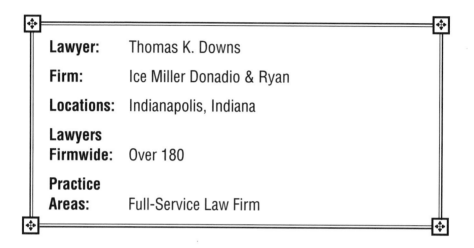

Lawyer: Thomas K. Downs

Firm: Ice Miller Donadio & Ryan

Locations: Indianapolis, Indiana

Lawyers
Firmwide: Over 180

Practice
Areas: Full-Service Law Firm

I practice in an area of the law that has seen a nation-wide falloff in business because of increased federal regulations over the past ten years. There has also been a general increase in competition during this time, resulting in reduced effective rates, gross revenues, and staffing cutbacks in prominent firms across the country. In addition, the practice area has been politicized to the extent that lawyers are sometimes chosen for reasons other than experience or capability. The area is municipal finance.

Over the course of those ten years, the practice group that I run has tripled or quadrupled gross revenues, increased effective rates, and expanded dramatically despite the loss of a major anchor client for political reasons.

How did we accomplish this? The stock (and accurate) answer is efficiency, quality of service, and competitiveness. More than that, the truth is that we love and live with our clients. We care about them as people and as friends, and we know about what they go through in the business of governing in the 1990s. Many lawyers will tell you that understanding your client's business and *accessibility* are two keys to success. I agree, but I have become so busy that I am frequently inaccessible for periods of time despite my best intentions. I wear a beeper, have a portable phone, and try to make myself available at virtually any hour of the day or night, but I am still hard to reach. My clients forgive me for this by and large because they know that I am out there caring for another client and that I will work through anything with them when needed. They also know that if I cannot get back to them, I will gauge their needs and make sure that a competent and responsive lawyer from our firm gets back to them promptly.

What does it mean to love and live with your clients? For one thing, it means devoting a great deal of time to them for which you can never charge. The time may be in doing pro bono work or it may be in attending a dinner honoring someone in a client's community or family. Nurturing clients means understanding their needs and their businesses but also knowing their families when appropriate and when they encourage it. You can be sure that you can't fake affection—I would never suggest that anybody try to make a career based on acting like they like a certain class of people or clients. Sooner or later that will catch up with you.

There are times when a client has a need that should be your highest priority and other times when clients are satisfied with someone else handling their matters. If they are negotiating the biggest deal of their life, or, in the municipal area, a deal that relates directly to their ability to serve another term, you had better make sure that is your highest priority. I cannot tell you how many times I have taken calls at home, or actually gone into the office to work on Thanks-giving or Christmas for a case where the priority was extremely high. I cannot tell you how many times I have worked until three or four o'clock in the morning. The next time around, however, that client is going to be exception-ally loyal to you and will tolerate your taking a certain amount of time getting a lower priority job done because they know you really do care about getting the job done.

It has always been my view that with friendship comes trust, and every lawyer will tell you that a relationship of trust with clients is essential. My further view is that with friendship and trust comes honesty. Clients with whom you have a relationship don't just ask you for your technical legal advice. They want your practical and business advice. The ethical rules on point focus on the lawyer as advisor or counselor. This relationship often requires you to tell a cli-ent something he or she doesn't want to hear. You can almost always tell beforehand that they are not going to want to hear a certain type of news. The key to the relation-ship is that through this friendship, trust, and honesty, you develop mutual respect. Therefore, they respect your views and make business decisions about whether to follow those views. In municipal finance practice, for better or worse, the bond lawyer must deliver an unqualified opinion about cer-tain matters in a transaction. Therefore, the ethical respon-sibilities of the bond lawyer are not only to help the issuer client achieve its goal but also to give an objective opinion to be relied on by a third party. Imagine the circumstances wherein clients really want to get something done and you tell them that it isn't legal and you can't give an opinion or that their deal won't have the positive benefits of the fed-eral tax exemption for municipal bonds. Imagine the bond issue where you tell them they have to disclose, under fed-eral securities law, something that may cost them money in their interest rates or embarrass their administration. Nonetheless, you must tell them the truth.

I have not yet lost any clients because I told them the truth or they couldn't do a deal the way they wanted. Of course, I never just tell them no. I tell them how the financing might be structured so that it will pass muster, or how they can go about getting the law changed so that we can accomplish their goals. As a corollary matter, I have not yet been fired because of a question about our fees. In fact, I can only remember a discussion about our fees in three or four financings over the past fifteen years, and those discussions were more about clarification than about the level of the fee. I firmly believe that the reason for this tolerance by our clients is that we have built up such trust and respect that they simply do not have any fears about our billing methods. In addition to that, when you work alongside clients in those high-priority deals until the wee hours of the morning, they pretty much know where you were and what you were billing them for and understand the sacrifices you have made to get them in the position in which they wanted to be.

I had one client that opened a simple general obligation bond file with us in 1979. The transaction evolved over the course of time into a $100 million plus railroad relocation. Ninety percent of the money came from federal funds and the mayor was able to leverage those funds until he actually had to issue bonds in 1994. There are those who would say that we lost money on our billing for the financing because of the present value of money and effective rate. However, this medium-sized Indiana city was one of our firm's top clients for two years running in the 1990s because they went through a tremendous period of growth that required infrastructure finance for a lot of other transactions during that period. Had we decided to "cut them off" because they really hadn't progressed on their bond issue for a period of ten or twelve years, we would not have had the type of relationship with them that led to their complete loyalty when they undertook their major capital plans.

I have a lot of local government clients that are very poor, rural, or both. I probably spent three years nurturing one county in its efforts to attract industry. Whether you call the time I spent business development or billable, the point is that there was no expectation of being paid unless the county was successful in its efforts. Despite that, I sympathized with a county that had suffered a tremendous loss of employment and where young people had to leave because there was no place to work. Numerous times I made the eight-hour round-trip drive to help them with public or private discussions about the need for economic development and to educate them about the tools they could use. I also helped them with several proposals to companies that chose other locations.

The good news is that on November 30, 1995, Toyota Motor Corporation chose this county as the site for a huge new plant. Everyone was happy and I think the county truly appreciates the fact that we were on their side before they were the fortunate recipient of this type of project. This is not an isolated incident. I have repeated it over and over with local governments and they all are very appreciative of the risk we take to help them improve themselves.

Our firm serves as counsel to the municipal and the county associations in Indiana. We donate well over $100,000 annually in pro bono time from very busy lawyers to assist those organizations. We are also always there when they need sponsorship or other financial assistance. One way to look at this is that it is simply business development. The way I look at it is that we have been very fortunate for decades to do this type of work and we owe it to give something back to the "community" of local governments. The bottom line is that the trust and loyalty and respect that we have is enhanced because of this further evidence of our commitment to understand and live with our clients.

I've heard the debate about whether the law is a business or a profession for a long time now. I am the only person I know of who teaches legal ethics and is a marketing partner for a big firm. To me, the debate is irrelevant. To do the right thing, you devote yourself to your clients and their interests, you disregard, or reject, opportunities to take shortcuts, and very good things happen. If you do this long enough, and you do it without compromise, your reputation will be assured and business will be there. You cannot, however, become complacent regardless of how good a reputation you've achieved and you must always take the long-term view of everything. Short-term planning is fine, and goal setting is necessary, but you always have to take a step back and think about what your short-term plans mean for the long-term best interests of your firm and, more importantly, your clients. If they don't prosper, you won't.

100 Percent Service . . .
100 Percent Referrals

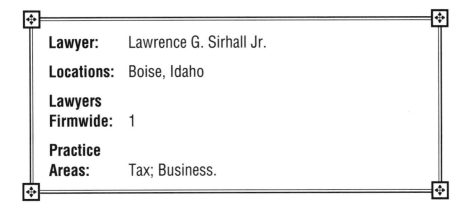

Lawyer: Lawrence G. Sirhall Jr.

Locations: Boise, Idaho

Lawyers Firmwide: 1

Practice Areas: Tax; Business.

I receive 100 percent of my new business from referrals. As a solo general practitioner, I have learned to rely on the word of mouth of satisfied clients to bring new clients into my practice. Many lawyers forget that ours is not only a profession but also a service industry. My ideas for effective client service include the following:

1. Return phone calls. I don't leave the office in the evening until every phone call is returned.
2. Be fair. Care about your clients. Be sincere. Be flexible. Be available when your clients need you.
3. Produce results. Remain focused on taking care of the needs of the client.
4. Don't charge for everything. Don't bill for every phone call. Do your share of pro bono work.

5. Be outgoing. Become active in your community. Participate in community events. Be friendly to people.

Overall, if you focus on satisfying and servicing the client, the rest takes care of itself.

The Service Guarantee

Lawyer: Ross H. Fishman

Firm: Coffield Ungaretti & Harris

Locations: Chicago, Illinois; Washington, D.C.

Lawyers Firmwide: Over 80

Practice Areas: General Practice; Business and Corporate; Financial Services and Securities; Litigation and Appeals; Real Estate; Health Care; Information Systems and Technology; Public Finance; Legislative Affairs and Government Relations; Labor and Employment; Employee Benefits; Environmental; Bankruptcy and Creditors' Rights; Estates and Trusts.

I am the marketing partner at Coffield Ungaretti & Harris, a ninety-lawyer Chicago law firm. Our law firm began guaranteeing our service and found it extremely useful not only in motivating tangible improvements to our client service but also in serving as a point of differentiation from our competitors. This year, when the profession grew by just 2 percent, our firm's revenues grew by more than 25 percent, much of this attributable to satisfying existing clients. The guarantee has also helped open doors to new contacts; we have found that contacts feel we are a safer choice than before.

Our guarantee is designed to enhance our clients' satisfaction with our service by ensuring that we are fully informed regarding their service needs. We only ask that at the earliest possible moment they inform us of any problems that may arise so that we have the immediate opportunity to address their concern.

Our guarantee states:

> We guarantee that as a client of Coffield, Ungaretti & Harris you will receive cost-effective legal services delivered in a timely manner. We promise to involve you and communicate with you regularly. We cannot guarantee outcomes; we do guarantee your satisfaction with our service. If Coffield Ungaretti & Harris does not perform to your satisfaction, inform us promptly. We will resolve the issue to your satisfaction, even if it means reducing your legal fees.

As you can see, if a client is not satisfied with our service, we will do whatever it takes to make it right, even if that means reducing our fees—short and simple. By putting the guarantee in writing, we want to emphasize our exceptional commitment to our clients.

We began our guarantee program because we found that sophisticated clients were moving their legal business to those firms that provide the highest quality service. We believed that the quality of service we already provided enabled us to guarantee our clients' satisfaction. We wanted to show the legal and business communities that we do indeed offer this level of attention and care. I believe that we were the first major law firm in the country to offer such a written guarantee.

Our clients have responded very favorably. If they are dissatisfied, we ask that they tell us promptly after the service is performed or other issues arise, so that we have the immediate opportunity to improve our service.

As Harvard professor Christopher W.I. Hart so aptly wrote in *The Power of Unconditional Service Guarantees*: "A guarantee will only work, of course, if you start with commitment to the customer."

This is precisely what Coffield Ungaretti & Harris has done. Our guarantee is structured to foster open and continuous communication with our clients. Through this process we will learn the way each client wants to be treated, which will help us to meet the client's identified standards. This solidifies relationships over the long term and enhances the service we provide to all of our clients.

This philosophy permeates through our entire firm. It is not enough for a firm to have *some* lawyers who provide high-quality service—the dedication to client service must be institutional, from top to bottom. We have that level of commitment.

The guarantee is our firm's latest step in a strategic, long-term commitment to improving the quality and efficiency of our service. Years ago the firm adopted a strategic plan to improve its competitiveness and the quality of service provided to its clients continually, conducted an in-depth client survey to discover client needs, implemented a $1.5 million cutting-edge information system to improve client service, and hired the nation's first client-service partner, and now we have implemented the nation's first law firm service guarantee.

Solve the Client's Problem

Lawyer: Laurie Burt

Firm: Foley, Hoag & Eliot

Locations: Boston, Massachusetts; Washington, D.C.

Lawyers
Firmwide: Over 150

Practice
Areas: Full-Service Law Firm

I am the chair of our firm's environmental practice. Lawyers who practice in the area of environmental law are often resourceful marketers because environmental law is a specialty area that has different dynamics than other practice areas. The practice is younger, very specialized, and highly competitive. To be successful, one has to learn how to attract and maintain clients of one's own and not rely solely on "internal" referrals from the traditional corporate or litigation practice groups.

I built my practice the old-fashioned way. I had to establish myself early on as a leader, a tough lawyer, and a creative problem solver. I began my career in the early 1970s, as an assistant attorney general when there were 120 cases at a time on my docket. I learned to develop a case strategy quickly and to pursue it aggressively. I also learned to be attentive to my client's needs and respectful of my opposing counsel no matter how intense the legal fight. In 1980 I moved into the private sector and built my environmental practice from scratch. I am very proud to say that our firm now has a group of fifteen lawyers practicing full-time in the environmental area.

The most sustaining and challenging aspect of my practice is when I can help my clients solve an environmental compliance problem creatively and cost-effectively. While many of my clients started out as clients with a specific environmental enforcement problem, I have been quick to introduce these clients to the benefits of compliance early on in the relationship. Cross-selling other individuals in our firm is important to achieving this because, in complying with environmental issues, a client often needs an experienced management protocol and an interdisciplinary team in the areas of intellectual property, international, tax, business, or real estate law. I formed an environmental business transaction team in our firm in 1985 that has been very successful in helping clients deal with these issues. Clients want to hire a lawyer who is a good risk manager as well as a skilled practitioner. This makes a creative approach. I generally will translate major cases for my clients into one or two key risk management issues that can be readily understood in business and practical terms. For most of my clients, a decision to buy, sell, clean up, or dispute an environmental claim is a huge decision with millions of dollars at risk. It is therefore imperative to be able to translate and calculate that risk for them. My personal marketing style consists of

- identifying the issues that separate the particular client from all others; and
- designing a strategy to meet the challenge creatively and cost-effectively.

I believe there are five sustaining principles that I have called upon over the years that have helped me move forward and enjoy truly productive, ever-expanding relationships with my clients, and I believe any lawyer could integrate these five principles into his or her practice.

1. **Vigilance.** You have to be ahead of the curve and engage in trying new things that can save your client money.
2. **Visibility.** Write articles and participate in interviews, CLE programs, or panel discussions. Be a leader and be known. Be able to foster and facilitate dialogue. Forge new ideas or pilot programs.
3. **Networking.** Make contacts! Make it your business to know key people affecting your practice area. Be sure to "tend" relationships and keep them going.
4. **Innovation.** Try new things. A lawyer today has to have a big toolbox full of new ideas to help achieve client's objectives and priorities. It takes a lot of problem-solving ability to be successful and maintain or expand your client base.
5. **Relationships.** Law is a relationship business. Know and attend to your clients. Know their priorities, objectives, and businesses. Listen to your clients and adhere to how they view the case and to what their needs are. I don't always tell my clients what they want to hear, but I make it my business to know my client's business. I do research on each client to enable me to gain a full understanding of their needs.

Above all else, I spend significant time with my clients reviewing the best and most relevant options. I view law as a service profession, and I like to hope that I demystify the legal and technical aspects of law and reduce the legal issues down to practical business terms. That is what clients need from a counselor. This type of communication is essential to establishing case priorities, realistic expectations, and successful results.

Put Clients First!

Our firm tried a number of different types of printed ads, but we found this approach to be too general. It didn't inspire clients or potential clients. Our most recent emphasis has been on a campaign to "Put Clients First!"

We initiated a client communication and audit program incorporating the following activities:

- We meet with our most active clients once a year for the purpose of finding out how we are doing and how we can improve our service.
- We call our clients at least once a quarter and thank them for their business. This *really* knocks their socks off.
- We are working toward initiating more of a client-focused culture within our law firm. Most of our lawyers are willing and eager to do anything that enhances relationships with clients. The remaining are slowly becoming more comfortable with the concept.

Our "core values" client program promotes quality, integrity, and teamwork.

Spencer Fane Britt & Browne started a "The Client Speaks" luncheon series, where our clients come and speak to an in-house team of lawyers about their businesses. We have had great success with this series, and it lets clients know we want to listen. It also brings our lawyers together and encourages teamwork, a concept that is foreign to many lawyers. We have become more knowledgeable about our clients through this effort and have established multiple links to our clients.

Our "Business Leaders" series has also proven very successful. We bring in business leaders to discuss their concerns in a variety of areas, such as employment, environmental, and real estate development issues.

At Spencer Fane Britt & Browne "University," we strive to bring clients and prospective clients into our office to help lawyers and staff learn about service. For example, a client may come in and talk about its corporate TQM program. We are working to form a client board of advisors, a brown-bag luncheon series, and client focus groups to help fulfill our commitment to teamwork.

Our firm has also started sponsoring a downtown athletic event for the local Boys & Girls Club. One hundred of our employees and fifty of our key clients joined together last year to make this event a success. The result of this has been the formation of stronger client ties through a common vision of commitment to our community.

E-Mail . . . A Client Service Link

Lawyer: Judith L. Grubner

Firm: Laff, Whitesel, Conte, & Saret, Ltd.

Locations: Chicago, Illinois

Lawyers Firmwide: 20

Practice Areas: Intellectual Property

I began using e-mail messaging to communicate with my clients in 1995, and have found that many clients are interested in utilizing this method to improve service and responsiveness. For me, initiating communication with my clients via e-mail was initially client-driven. I had a client who was interested in receiving an "instant response" to his questions and requested that I use e-mail rather than facsimile communication because he could receive drafts right at his desk. We had previously tried exchanging disks and modem transmission but ran into problems because he preferred to use a Macintosh computer. We were preparing agreements for his intellectual property needs and soon discovered that through the use of e-mail, we could work on the documents together to make nearly instant decisions about modifications. I kept copies of the client's agreements on my computer as e-mail documents and the client did likewise. This facilitated communication between the two of us and made it possible for me to actually *show* the client changes to the agreements on the screen, as he preferred. Today, I find that I am using e-mail communication more and more with my clients. When I get a new client, I routinely ask, "Do you have e-mail capability?," and I believe this is something that distinguishes me from many other lawyers. I also believe that by reviewing documents directly on e-mail, my clients can respond to me with greater ease. For example, we have several clients in Hawaii, and given the time difference, we have found that e-mail is a very good alternative to phone calls at odd hours. The clients don't have to be so cognizant of my schedule, and can send me changes to documents at *their* convenience, even when I am not immediately available. My clients appreciate this convenience, and I find that I am receiving additional business from them because I am "e-mail friendly." My initial "e-mail client" now gives me more business because I can provide him with a quicker response and at the same time save him money. We find that we spend a lot less time trading messages on the phone now that we rely on our e-mail capability. In previous years, I averaged three agreements per year from this client, and I am now being given as many as three agreements *per month*.

Overall, using e-mail as a tool has increased my efficiency, and has created a cost savings for my clients. I plan to continue using e-mail as a marketing tool and am pleased to say that a number of other lawyers in my firm are also experimenting with e-mail to serve clients. To date, all clients are extremely satisfied!

PART 5

Referrals: Making a Name for Yourself

The Ripple Effect

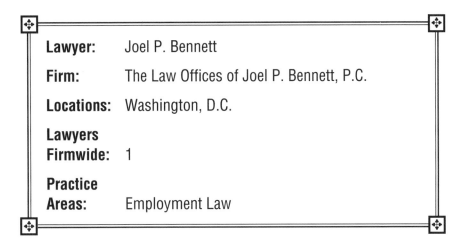

Lawyer: Joel P. Bennett

Firm: The Law Offices of Joel P. Bennett, P.C.

Locations: Washington, D.C.

Lawyers Firmwide: 1

Practice Areas: Employment Law

My marketing philosophy is based on years of experience with the "ripple effect." If you throw pebbles into the water, this results in ripples, which result in more ripples, and so on. The more pebbles you throw, the more ripples you get. Clients are like ripples. With clients, the more contacts you initiate, the more clients you generate.

Name recognition is important to the ripple effect. Referrals can come from the most unusual places. My suggestions for building name recognition include the following three:

1. Make sure to connect your name with an area of practice. I created a specialty area of practice for myself in employment law, and within five years, this was the vast majority of my practice. My success

is partially owed to writing for the ABA and local bar associations. I have written or edited three books as well as many articles, which has created a ripple effect for me. Now over half of my business comes from referrals from other lawyers.

2. Get out and meet people. I have done this through a number of approaches but have had great success with being active in local bar groups. My practice is essentially local, and I rarely have a matter that goes beyond fifty miles from my office. I am actively involved in three main groups, including serving as president of the voluntary Bar Association of the District of Columbia, which has been in existence for more than 125 years, as well as being active in the mandatory District of Columbia Bar, which has more than 66,000 members. I have generated many referrals from these groups.

3. Always create a favorable impression. When you are involved in professional or community groups, make it a point to become active. Don't miss meetings. Meet deadlines. Deliver on your promises. In turn, you will have work referred to you. Other lawyers will refer clients to you if you have impressed them. Don't unnecessarily alienate opposing counsel. I get many referrals from lawyers practicing in big law firms. Why do they refer business to me? First, they believe that I am competent. Second, in my experience with them, I did not alienate them. I try to be a zealous advocate for my client without being uncivil to opposing counsel and judges.

Overall, through my involvement, I have created my own ripple effect. I have learned that business can come to you in the strangest ways. You have to make a name for yourself. I have never done any media advertising, but I do send press releases to local and legal media, and I make it a point to write and speak on a regular basis.

In October 1996 I celebrated my twentieth anniversary as a solo practitioner. Throughout my career, I estimate that most of my business has been from referrals. More than 50 percent of these referrals have come from other lawyers, 10 percent have come from people who have heard me speak directly, and the rest have been from referrals from other individuals and clients. The key is to get out there and meet people to create your own "ripple effect."

Marketing by Reputation—
The People's Law Firm

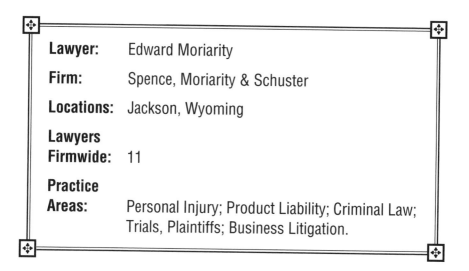

Lawyer: Edward Moriarity

Firm: Spence, Moriarity & Schuster

Locations: Jackson, Wyoming

**Lawyers
Firmwide:** 11

**Practice
Areas:**   Personal Injury; Product Liability; Criminal Law;
Trials, Plaintiffs; Business Litigation.

My partner since 1974 has been Gerry Spence. With Gerry, you don't have to market. We have an interesting story to share. Our law firm was created in 1974, as Spence & Moriarity, and we now enjoy a unique reputation—because Gerry has built this reputation over the past twenty-five years.

I can only describe Gerry Spence as a genius. He is a very smart and extremely articulate person. Above all, he is able to communicate effectively with *all* people. Over the years, although we have achieved a national reputation and a great deal of notoriety, we have had to work extremely hard. Gerry Spence has trained everyone in our office to work hard. We prepare cases down to the most minute detail, and we achieve good results.

Our marketing strategy is simple. We decided early on not to take cases in our hometown and to represent only people, not large corporations. We actually began our firm in Casper, Wyoming, but after four years we could not even go to a doctor in town because we had sued so many of them. We learned our lesson, and by 1978 we had relocated our offices from Casper to Jackson, Wyoming. Now we don't get involved in local disputes because our quality of life is important to us.

Thanks to Gerry's direction and the hard work of the other lawyers in the firm, we have built a strong reputation. Before the formation of Spence, Moriarity & Schuster, Gerry was recognized for providing unmatched representation for insurance companies in the Northwest. Then, suddenly, he changed his direction. Gerry was in a local grocery store and met a plaintiff who he had won a lawsuit against on behalf of a large insurance company. The man was crippled and recognized Gerry as the lawyer who had won the case against him. The man looked at Gerry and said that he did not resent Gerry for his situation and that he thought Gerry was a very competent lawyer. Gerry was very touched by his meeting with this man and went back to his office and wrote a letter to all his insurance company clients informing them that he could no longer represent big companies. He wanted to represent people. Since that time we have only represented people, not corporations or banks, just people.

Representing people has served as the basis for our firm for the past two decades. Gerry got his first real national exposure when he won the $10.5 million verdict against Kerr McGee for Karen Silkwood's survivors. That was the case that put Gerry in the limelight. A verdict of that magnitude was unheard of in the late 1970s, and Gerry went on to recover $26.5 million from *Penthouse* magazine on behalf of a girl who had been Miss Wyoming, who the jury believed had been defamed by *Penthouse*. Gerry and our firm also won a $52 million jury verdict against McDonald's Corporation for a small ice cream company. We were certainly on the map after these successes.

As we were more and more successful, we received more and more calls from individuals desiring representation. We also got a lot of our cases as a result of referrals from other lawyers. Our firm is still small, we have ten lawyers, but we receive between five hundred and seven hundred calls a month from people wanting representation. Gerry has not lost a trial since 1969, and people want him to help them win.

In thinking about our success, I believe we owe our success to three things:

1. Working very hard.
2. Maintaining the good reputation that we have earned.
3. Achieving good results for our clients.

Gerry Spence may be one of the most famous lawyers in America, but he is also one of the hardest working people that I know. He takes his profession very seriously and it shows. He has represented everyone from Imelda Marcos to your average person, and has even sued the United States government and won, but his success is not due to any magic. It is all because of hard work.

Today, we accept about 1 percent of the potential cases that we receive, only because we have limited resources to provide effective representation for everyone. We have a meeting three times a week to discuss potential new cases. We refer a lot of cases out and maintain the policy that we always look out for the best interest of the client. We get "social" returns from our work—it is not a matter of making a large sum of money. We don't accept cases unless they have some underlying social justice. We feel so strongly about social justice, that we have established a public inter-est group to handle these types of cases. Presently, the Public Interest Law Firm is active in Wyoming, but we are hoping to expand this to a national level soon.

Gerry Spence also began a trial lawyers' college at his ranch in Wyoming. The college brings in fifty trial lawyers a year to train them to be better attorneys. The major requirement is that these lawyers must represent people. We have set up a scholarship program for the trial lawyers' college and Gerry donates money from the proceeds of the sale of his books to finance some of it.

Overall, I would stress that our marketing is now a result of the reputation we have earned over the past two decades. We continue to strive to achieve a social justice and will continue in this effort throughout the coming years. It's all in building a good reputation, whether it is on a local, national, or international level, and working hard to main-tain that reputation over the years. Success is nothing with-out hard work!

Ask for the Order!

<table>
<tr><td>Lawyer:</td><td>Donald P. Knudsen</td></tr>
<tr><td>Firm:</td><td>Gunderson, Palmer, Goodsell & Nelson, L.L.P.</td></tr>
<tr><td>Locations:</td><td>Rapid City, South Dakota</td></tr>
<tr><td>Lawyers Firmwide:</td><td>10</td></tr>
<tr><td>Practice Areas:</td><td>General Civil Trial Practice; State and Federal Appeals; Banking; Commercial and Insurance Litigation; Contracts; Corporations; Creditors' Rights in Bankruptcy; Gaming; Insurance; Personal Injury; Probate; Real Estate; Natural Resources; Surety Law; Family Law; Administrative Law; Estate Planning; Public Financing; Elder Law; Limited Liability Companies; Tax Law.</td></tr>
</table>

My practice is still developing, and I am gradually building an ongoing client base after eight years of practice. I began practicing in a geographic area in South Dakota where I had no "natural" contacts because I had not grown up there. To make some contacts, I became involved in social groups, a country club, the YMCA, Leadership Rapid City, a service club, and my church. I had an active involvement in these organizations, and I let everyone possible know that I was a lawyer. I realized that it takes time for people to get to know you, and after eight years, my practice is starting to mushroom because of this visibility. I am now starting to get my name in the paper once in a while, which helps establish me as an expert in my practice area (employment law). I am getting referrals from other lawyers who are recognizing me as a lawyer they can trust to do a good job for a client. However, being known and active in the community is not enough.

You have to ask for the order. I let the people I meet know that I would be honored to do their legal work. My partners and I do a wide range of other marketing activities. We have a Yellow Pages ad and have done a very tasteful television commercial, which has generated some business for us. We speak at seminars and have the largest Christmas party in town, but I am convinced that you cannot be successful unless you first ask for the order, deliver quality service, return phone calls, send regular status reports, and then thank clients for their business. Every time I receive a referral from someone, I send them a thank-you note. It takes two minutes. Guess what? They send referral after referral.

In the Traffic

Lawyer:	Raquel A. Rodriguez
Firm:	Greenberg Traurig
Locations:	Miami, Florida; Fort Lauderdale, Florida; West Palm Beach, Florida; Orlando, Florida; Tallahassee, Florida; New York, New York; Washington, D.C.
Lawyers Firmwide:	Over 250
Practice Areas:	Full-Service Law Firm

My marketing strategy is to get to know as many people as possible and build personal relationships with them. My involvement in the ABA has been a great start. I consistently try to meet and befriend as many people as possible. I am naturally an outgoing person and enjoy people, and for me this translates into good marketing. You have to stay in the traffic and be in places to get to know people who can refer business to you. You never know where a referral will come from. One particular story comes to mind.

A potential client involved in a litigation matter was recommended to our firm. After an initial consultation, this client ended up using a small firm, but I was persistent about staying in touch just to check up on him and see how the case was progressing. I took a personal interest in the client, and at one point he asked me to evaluate the work done by his lawyer and to represent him in certain key aspects of the case.

I know that eventually because of my personal interest in the client he will bring *all* of his legal work over to our firm. I focus on building personal relationships, staying in the traffic, providing good service, and supporting these efforts by writing, speaking, and participating in CLE seminars.

Community
Involvement Counts

Lawyer: Lowell E. Rothschild

Firm: Meseh, Clark & Rothschild P.C.

Locations: Tucson, Arizona

Lawyers Firmwide: 14

Practice Areas: General Civil and Trial Practice in All State and Federal Courts; Probate; Insurance; Negligence; Utility; Corporation; Bankruptcy; Trials.

After forty-four years of practicing law, I have been convinced that to attract clients you must actively market yourself. You have to "sell" your strengths. For me, community involvement became very key. Early in my career, I became active in community organizations, including the Cystic Fibrosis Foundation, the American Cancer Society, the University of Arizona Alumni Association and Foundation, the Tucson Airport Authority, and my temple, and actively supported the organization's causes. This enabled me to give something back to the community and not be viewed as somebody who was just a taker. Community involvement also enables people to see a side of a lawyer that they don't normally see. I developed relationships with the media—print, radio, and television—and made a very special effort to contribute articles or quotes as often as possible to the daily newspapers. I scheduled lunches with key reporters to review new legal developments to assist them in better understanding the legal aspects of the stories they were writing. The newspapers, thereafter, called me as their "source."

Networking with other lawyers is important. I recommend becoming active in your specialty section of the bar and networking with other professionals, including physicians, CPAs, and general practice lawyers.

Periodically, our firm would sponsor breakfasts and dinner seminar meetings to offer these professionals something proactive that they could use in their practice and to get to know them and gain exposure with them. Through these activities, my expertise in my specialty, bankruptcy and debtor-creditor relationships, became well-known and my name was constantly before possible referrers.

The Political Arena

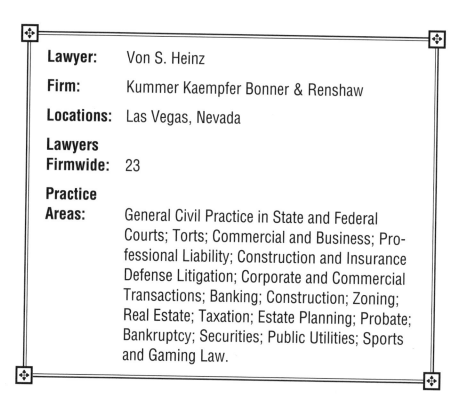

Lawyer: Von S. Heinz

Firm: Kummer Kaempfer Bonner & Renshaw

Locations: Las Vegas, Nevada

Lawyers Firmwide: 23

Practice Areas: General Civil Practice in State and Federal Courts; Torts; Commercial and Business; Professional Liability; Construction and Insurance Defense Litigation; Corporate and Commercial Transactions; Banking; Construction; Zoning; Real Estate; Taxation; Estate Planning; Probate; Bankruptcy; Securities; Public Utilities; Sports and Gaming Law.

I have found the ABA political arena to be a rewarding source of business. Over the past decade, I have been involved with the steering committees of several candidates running for ABA division and national offices and have even been a candidate myself on a couple of occasions (regrettably unsuccessfully). Each political venture has given me new contacts and promoted business for me and my firm.

Regardless of whether you are the candidate or someone working to achieve another volunteer's election, here are some tips on how to use the political arena as a business-generating enterprise for you.

1. Make sure you put your best foot forward at all times. Throughout the course of the campaign, you are going to encounter old acquaintances and make new ones, some of whom will be your supporters and others who will not. Whether you are the candidate or the representative embodiment of your candidate, you need to approach everyone with the same degree of basic respect and civility. Like clients, people often make voting decisions after a lengthy evaluation of the individual and how he or she treats and is received by others.

2. Run your race with a view toward your next election. Think of how many times parties on the other side of a lawsuit or against whom you are negotiating call you to represent them on their next legal matter. "The next time I'm going to hire that lawyer." This marketing strategy applies equally in the political arena. For reasons beyond your control, you may not be someone's candidate today, but earn their respect and you may find that person in your support column next time.

3. Do not be afraid to take a political stand. People endorse candidates the same way they choose their lawyers. They look for integrity, energy, commitment, and the ability to take on an issue and argue forcefully for it. Demonstrating these skills in the political sphere will encourage others to translate those abilities to how you would perform as a lawyer, for them and their clients. Be at your best, exercise common sense and decorum, and speak convincingly and with conviction, especially on issues where others are likely to disagree with you.

4. Make sure others recognize your appreciation. Treat your campaign like a client, by remembering to plan ahead, to keep your volunteers advised and make them part of the decision-making process, and to express your thanks for their efforts frequently and sincerely. The same skills we are taught to demonstrate with our clients (e.g., prompt acknowledgment of telephone calls, following through on promised obligations) will help others see the best of your lawyering skills.

Political activism has brought me referrals from all areas of the country, including business from an international beverage manufacturing and distributing corporation; a national department store chain; and a wide number of individuals and businesses seeking to take advantage of the favorable business climate in Nevada for corporate activities. It has been fascinating to note, too, that I have had as many referrals from my political "foes" as from my "allies." My contacts have also serviced my firm's clients. When a client needs to be referred to a lawyer in New Haven or Knoxville, for example, I can make a recommendation based on personal knowledge of that lawyer's individual skills that will be of benefit to the client's interest.

Become Distinguished

Lawyer: Brewster H. Jamieson

Firm: Lane Powell Spears Lubersky

Locations: Anchorage, Alaska; Fairbanks, Alaska; Seattle, Washington; Mount Vernon, Washington; Olympia, Washington; Los Angeles, California; San Francisco, California; Portland, Oregon; London, England

Lawyers Firmwide: Over 250

Practice Areas: General Practice and Litigation in Federal and State Courts and before Federal and State Administrative Tribunals; Admiralty and Maritime; Alternative Dispute Resolution; Antitrust; Appellate Practice; Aviation; Banking and Financial Institutions; Bankruptcy and Reorganizations; Communications and Media; Construction and Engineering; Corporate and Corporate Finance; Emerging Companies; Employee Benefits; Environmental; Forest Products and Natural Resources; Hospital and Health Care; Immigration; Insurance; Intellectual Property and Computer Law; International Transactions; Labor Relations and Employment; Municipal Law and Municipal Finance; Public Utility and Energy Law; Real Estate and Land Use; Retailing; Securities; Taxation; Toxic Torts; Transportation; Trusts and Estates; Venture Capital; White-Collar Criminal Law.

I believe that the most unique thing about my marketing effort is the fact that my geographic location is Alaska. I have a very broad-based litigation practice, with an emphasis in maritime law.

I grew up in Alaska, then went to Seattle in 1985 and worked with a large firm. In 1990 I returned to Alaska. The most interesting thing about practicing law here is the remoteness. I have always had a commitment to provide excellent service to my clients, so I spend a great deal of my free time on airplanes, traveling to visit them. It is an automatic three hours by plane to get to a major city in the United States, and by the time you add in the travel time to and from the airport, it usually takes six hours for me to get to Seattle, the closest major city. My clients are spread out all over the world. The remoteness of Alaska makes it doubly challenging to provide excellent service, but I make a special point to do whatever it takes to meet the demands of my clients. If I am working with a client in Japan, I end up staying late in the office to accommodate the time difference. If I have a case in the United Kingdom, I go in early so that I am available if the client calls. I time my correspondence so that it arrives in the client's office at the opening of the business day. If I am traveling for client meetings, I try to plan ahead and take an extra day to play golf or have some social time with my clients and contacts in that location. The key to good service is that you have to be available to deliver the goods. I spend a lot of time using my laptop computer and picking up my e-mail and voice mail remotely. Keeping in touch with clients when I am on the road is vital to my practice.

Our entire firm is based on this quality service theme. Because of this commitment to service, we are finding that over 80 percent of our new business is coming from existing clients through referrals. Word of mouth is a very powerful marketing tool.

To maintain these client relationships effectively, one thing that I do every year is send out more than five hundred Christmas cards to clients and contacts. I take the time to write a personal note in each one. This is something that distinguishes me from the crowd, and I have never had a client be offended by receiving a card. Just living in Alaska also distinguishes me from the crowd. It is a bit of a novelty. People are naturally fascinated by the state. Living up here, I have lots of tales to tell, most of which are true, and many of which are humorous. I use "moose stories" to entertain my clients and have sent them photos that I have taken of moose interacting with my pets or looking right at me from my back deck. One client even proudly displays my moose photo in his living room! A few years ago, we had a really bad winter, with heavy snowfall. A photograph was featured in the local paper of a moose standing on top of a roof eating tree branches, so I cut it out and sent it to a client. There is a serious side to the moose issue, however. People are sometimes killed or seriously injured by moose, and I have even had cases involving collisions between cars and moose. In New York, they have their rats, and in Alaska, we have our moose. Stories about Alaska, its wildlife, and its unique people give my clients and contacts something to remember me by, which in turn gives me a marketing advantage!

Selected Books From...

LPM PUBLISHING

ABA Guide to Lawyer Trust Accounts. This book deals with how lawyers should manage trust accounts to comply with ethical & statutory requirements.

ABA Guide to Professional Managers in the Law Office. This book provides guidelines that show how professional management can and does work. It shows lawyers how to practice more efficiently by delegating management tasks to professional managers.

Becoming Computer Literate. A guide to computer basics for lawyers and other legal professionals.

Billing Innovations. This book looks at Innovative fee arrangements and how your approach toward billing can deeply affect the attorney-client relationship. It also explains how billing and pricing are absolutely intertwined with strategic planning, maintaining quality of services, marketing, instituting a compensation system, and firm governance.

Changing Jobs, 2nd Ed. A handbook designed to help lawyers make changes in their professional careers. Includes career planning advice from nearly 50 experts.

Compensation Plans for Law Firms, 2nd Ed. This second edition discusses the basics for a fair and simple compensation system for partners, of counsel, associates, paralegals, and staff.

Connecting with Your Client. Written by a psychologist, therapist, and legal consultant, this book presents communications techniques that will help ensure client cooperation and satisfaction.

Do-It-Yourself Public Relations. A hands-on guide for lawyers with public relations ideas, sample letters and forms. The book includes a diskette that includes model letters to the press that have paid off in news stories and media attention.

Finding the Right Lawyer. This guide answers the questions people should ask when searching for legal counsel. It includes a glossary of legal specialties and the ten questions you should ask a lawyer before hiring.

Flying Solo: A Survival Guide for the Solo Lawyer, 2nd ed. An updated and expanded guide to the problems and issues unique to the solo practitioner.

How to Draft Bills Clients Rush to Pay. A collection of techniques for drafting bills that project honesty, competence, fairness and value and how draft an inviting statement.

How to Start and Build a Law Practice, 3rd ed. Jay Foonberg's classic guide has been updated and expanded. Included are more than 10 new chapters on marketing, financing, automation, practicing from home, ethics and professional responsibility.

Law Office Policy and Procedures Manual, 3rd edition. This book provides a model for law office policies and procedures. It covers such topics as law office organization, management, administration, personnel policies and benefits, office security and emergency procedures, financial management, technology, and communications systems.

The Lawyer's Guide to the Internet. A no-nonsense guide to what the Internet is (and isn't), how it applies to the legal profession, and the different ways it can -- and should -- be used.

The Lawyer's Guide to Marketing on the Internet. This book talks about the pluses and minuses of marketing on the Internet, as well as how to develop an Internet marketing plan.

Leaders' Digest: A Review of the Best Books on Leadership. This book will help you find the best books on leadership to help you achieve extraordinary and exceptional leadership skills.

Leveraging with Legal Assistants. This book reviews the changes that have led to increased use of legal assistants and the need to enlarge their role further. Learn specific ways in which a legal assistant can handle a substantial portion of traditional lawyer work.

Living with the Law: Strategies to Avoid Burnout and Create Balance. This multi-author book is intended to help lawyers manage stress, make the practice of law more satisfying, and improve client service.

Microsoft® Word for Windows in One Hour for Lawyers. This book includes special tips for users of Windows 95. It contains four easy lessons--timed at 15 minutes each--that will help lawyers prepare, save, and edit a basic document.

Practicing Law Without Clients: Making a Living as a Freelance Lawyer. This book describes the freelance legal researching, writing, and consulting opportunities that are available to lawyers

Results-Oriented Financial Management. A Guide to Successful Law Firm Financial Performance. How to manage "the numbers," from setting rates and computing billable hours to calculating net income and preparing the budget. Over 30 charts and statements to help you prepare reports.

Survival Guide for Road Warriors. A guide to using a notebook computer and combinations of equipment and technology so lawyers can be effective in their office, on the road, in the courtroom or at home.

Through the Client's Eyes. Includes an overview of client relations and sample letters, surveys, and self-assessment questions to gauge your client relations acumen.

Women Rainmakers' 101+ Best Marketing Tips. A collection of over 130 marketing tips suggested by women rainmakers throughout the country. Includes tips on image, networking, public relations, and advertising.

WordPerfect® 101 for the Law Office AND WordPerfect® 201 for the Law Office. These two guides are for the new and intermediate WordPerfect 6.1 user. Volume 1 reviews creating, editing and saving documents. While Volume 2 delves into advanced editing and automation features. Each volume includes exercises on diskettes. Sold separately.

WordPerfect® 6.1 for Windows in One Hour for Lawyers. This is a crash course in the most popular word processing software package used by lawyers. In four lessons, you'll learn the basic steps for getting a simple job done.

LPM PUBLISHING
Order Form

Qty	Title	LPM Price	Regular Price	Total
_____	ABA Guide to Lawyer Trust Accounts (5110374)	$ 69.95	$ 79.95	$_____
_____	ABA Guide to Prof. Managers in the Law Office (5110373)	69.95	79.95	$_____
_____	Becoming Computer Literate (5110342)	32.95	39.95	$_____
_____	Billing Innovations (5110366)	124.95	144.95	$_____
_____	Changing Jobs, 2nd Ed. (5110334)	49.95	59.95	$_____
_____	Compensation Plans for Lawyers (5110353)	69.95	79.95	$_____
_____	Connecting with Your Client (5110378)	54.95	64.95	$_____
_____	Do-It-Yourself Public Relations (5110352)	69.95	79.95	$_____
_____	Finding the Right Lawyer (5110339)	19.95	19.95	$_____
_____	Flying Solo, 2nd Ed. (5110328)	59.95	69.95	$_____
_____	How to Draft Bills Clients Rush to Pay (5110344)	39.95	49.95	$_____
_____	How to Start & Build a Law Practice, 3rd Ed. (5110293)	32.95	39.95	$_____
_____	Law Office Policy & Procedures Manual (5110375)	99.95	109.95	$_____
_____	Lawyer's Guide to the Internet (5110343)	24.95	29.95	$_____
_____	Lawyer's Guide to Marketing on the Internet (5110371)	54.95	64.95	$_____
_____	Leaders' Digest (5110356)	49.95	59.95	$_____
_____	Leveraging with Legal Assistants (5110322)	59.95	69.95	$_____
_____	Living with the Law (5110379)	59.95	69.95	$_____
_____	Microsoft Word for Windows in One Hour (5110358)	19.95	29.95	$_____
_____	Practicing Law Without Clients (5110376)	49.95	59.95	$_____
_____	Results-Oriented Financial Management (5110319)	44.95	54.95	$_____
_____	Survival Guide for Road Warriors (5110362)	24.95	29.95	$_____
_____	Through the Client's Eyes (5110337)	69.95	79.95	$_____
_____	Women Rainmakers' 101+ Best Marketing Tips (5110336)	14.95	19.95	$_____
_____	WordPerfect® 101 for the Law Office (5110364)	59.95	64.95	$_____
_____	WordPerfect® 201 for the Law Office (5110365)	59.95	64.95	$_____
_____	WordPerfect® 101 & 201 Package (5110369)	89.90	99.90	$_____
_____	WordPerfect® 6.1 for Windows in One Hour for Lawyers (5110354)	19.95	29.95	$_____

*HANDLING
$10.00-$24.99 ... $3.95
$25.00-$49.99 ... $4.95
$50.00+ $5.95

**TAX
DC residents add 5.75%
IL residents add 8.75%
MD residents add 5%

SUBTOTAL: $_____
*HANDLING: $_____
**TAX: $_____
TOTAL: $_____

PAYMENT
☐ Check enclosed (to the ABA)   ☐ Bill Me   ☐ Visa   ☐ MasterCard   ☐ American Express

Account Number:_____Exp. Date: _____

Signature_____

Name_____

Firm_____

Address_____

City_____State_____ZIP_____

Phone number_____

Mail to: ABA Publication Orders
           P.O. Box 10892
           Chicago, IL 60610-0892

Phone: (800) 285-2221   Fax: (312) 988-5568

Email: abasvcctr@abanet.org   World Wide Web: http//www.abanet.org/lpm/catalog

Source Code: BOC

THE SECTION OF
LAW PRACTICE
MANAGEMENT

CUSTOMER COMMENT FORM

Title of Book:_____

We've tried to make this publication as useful, accurate, and readable as possible. Please take 5 minutes to tell us if we succeeded. Your comments and suggestions will help us improve our publications. Thank you!

1. How did you acquire this publication:

☐ by mail-order   ☐ at a meeting/convention   ☐ as a gift

☐ by phone order   ☐ at a bookstore   ☐ don't know

☐ other: (describe)_____

Please rate this publication as follows:

	Excellent	Good	Fair	Poor	Not Applicable
Readability: Was the book easy to read and understand?	☐	☐	☐	☐	☐
Examples/cases: Were they helpful, practical? Were there enough?	☐	☐	☐	☐	☐
Content: Did the book meet your expectations? Did it cover the subject adequately?	☐	☐	☐	☐	☐
Organization and clarity: Was the sequence of text logical? Was it easy to find what you wanted to know?	☐	☐	☐	☐	☐
Illustrations/forms/checklists: Were they clear and useful? Were there enough?	☐	☐	☐	☐	☐
Physical attractiveness: What did you think of the appearance of the publication (typesetting, printing, etc.)?	☐	☐	☐	☐	☐

Would you recommend this book to another lawyer/administrator?   ☐ Yes   ☐ No

How could this publication be improved? What else would you like to see in it?

_____

_____

_____

Do you have other comments or suggestions?_____

_____

_____

Name_____

Firm/Company_____

Address_____

City/State/ZIP_____ Phone_____

Firm Size_____ Area of concentration_____

We appreciate your time and help.

Fold

BUSINESS REPLY MAIL
FIRST CLASS   PERMIT NO. 16471   CHICAGO, ILLINOIS

POSTAGE WILL BE PAID BY ADDRESSEE

AMERICAN BAR ASSOCIATION
PPM, 8TH FLOOR
750 N. LAKE SHORE DRIVE
CHICAGO, ILLINOIS 60611-9851

Fold

AMERICAN BAR ASSOCIATION

SECTION OF LAW PRACTICE MANAGEMENT
MEMBERSHIP APPLICATION

Access to all these information resources and discounts – for just $2.92 a month!

Membership dues are just $35 a year – just $2.92 a month.
You probably spend more on your general business magazines and newspapers.
But they can't help you succeed in building and managing your practice like LPM.
Make a small investment in success. Join today!

☑ **Yes!** I want to join the Section of Law Practice Management and gain access to information helping me add more clients, retain and expand business with current clients, and run my law practice more efficiently and competitively!

Check the dues that apply to you:
❏ $35 for ABA members   ❏ $5 for ABA Law Student Division members

Choose your method of payment:
❏ Check enclosed (make payable to American Bar Association)
❏ Bill me
❏ Charge to my: ❏ VISA®   ❏ MASTERCARD®   ❏ AMEX®

Card No.: _____ Exp. Date: _____

Signature: _____ Date: _____

ABA I.D.*: _____
(* *Please note: Membership in ABA is a prerequisite to enroll in ABA Sections.*)

Name: _____

Firm/Organization: _____

Address: _____

City/State/ZIP: _____

Telephone No.: _____ Fax No.: _____

Primary Email Address: _____

Save time by Faxing or Phoning!
▶ Fax your application to: (312) 988-5820
▶ Join by phone if using a credit card: (800) 285-2221 (ABA1)
▶ Email us for more information at: lpm@attmail.com
▶ Check us out on the Internet: http://www.abanet.org/lpm/org

> **GUARANTEED SATISFACTION:**
> Your membership must save you time, must give you the edge you need to thrive in the increasingly competitive law business – just as it does for our other 20,000 members. However, if for any reason, at anytime, you think we're not working for you, cancel your membership and receive a refund on the unused portion of your membership.

I understand that Section dues include a $24 basic subscription to Law Practice Management; this subscription charge is not deductible from the dues and additional subscriptions are not available at this rate. Membership dues in the American Bar Association are not deductible as charitable contributions for income tax purposes. However, such dues may be deductible as a business expense.

THE SECTION OF
LAW PRACTICE
MANAGEMENT
750 N. LAKE SHORE DRIVE
CHICAGO, IL 60611
PHONE: (312) 988-5619
FAX: (312) 988-5820
Email: lpm@attmail.com

Membership Application